EVERYTHING
TASTES
BETTER
WITH BACON

# EVERYTHING TASTES BETTER WITH BACON

70 Fabulous Recipes for
Every Meal of the Day

by Sara Perry

Photographs by Sheri Giblin

CHRONICLE BOOKS

SAN FRANCISCO

Library of Congress Cataloging-in-Publication Data:

Perry, Sara.
    Everything tastes better with bacon : 70 fabulous
    recipes for every meal of the day / by Sara Perry.
        p.        cm.
    Includes index.
    ISBN 0-8118-3239-2 (pbk.)
    1. Cookery (Pork) 2. Bacon I. Title.
    TX749 .P48 2001
    641.6'64—dc21
    2001037240

Manufactured in China.

Prop styling by Sara Slavin
Food styling by Erin Quon and Kim Konecny
Photo assistant: Tiffany Schoepp
Design and typesetting by Open, NY
Illustrations by Chip Wass

Distributed in Canada by Raincoast Books
9050 Shaughnessy Street
Vancouver, BC V6P 6E5

10 9 8 7 6 5 4 3 2 1

Chronicle Books LLC
85 Second Street
San Francisco, California 94105
www.chroniclebooks.com

## TO BILL LeBLOND

Everything goes better with Bill.
He's a gem to work for, a pleasure to be with,
and a kind and loyal friend.

## Acknowledgments

Thanks go to the friends and colleagues who
generously shared their ideas, expertise, time,
and recipes, especially Jane Zwinger, Suzy Kitman,
Mittie Hellmich, Sharon Maasdam, Linda Faes,
Kathlyn and Matthew Meskel, Karen Brooks, Susan
Friedland, Arlene Schnitzer, chef Kenny Giambalvo,
pastry chef Jennifer Welshhons, pastry chef
Debbie Putnam, Amy Treadwell at Chronicle Books,
and Frank Everett, whose taste for bacon is an
inspiration. To Kris Balloun, whose copy editing
was superb and just this side of miraculous. And to
Catherine Glass, whose confidence and advice are
always invaluable.

# CONTENTS

ACHIN' FOR BACON

# EVERYTHING TASTES BETTER WITH BACON.
# WELL, *ALMOST* EVERYTHING.

**IN THE MORNING,** the sound and smell of bacon cooking in the skillet give me the feeling that I have time. I can relax and savor the day. Wonderful to share, bacon is also the quintessential comfort food when you're alone. The reason goes to the essence of what bacon is and maybe even to its ancient role as the food that took whole families through the winter. When cornflakes won't do it and bagels seem boring, try Daddy's Fluffy Scrambled Eggs with Bacon, Sweetie-Pie Pancake with Brown Sugar Apples and Bacon, or Brie and Bacon Frittata.

If you haven't had bacon for breakfast (or even if you have), there's always lunch. A hamburger tastes so much better as a bacon cheeseburger, and a BLT without bacon is nothing more than salad and toast. Bacon makes these classic icons. Same goes for the Club Sandwich, the Kentucky Hot Brown, and the Cobb Salad, which you'll also find in this book. But bacon enhances other not-so-familiar but oh-so-tasty recipes, too. Warm Potato Salad with Bacon and Arugula is just the thing for a family reunion, and Risotto with Spicy Pepper Bacon and Marsala is a great winter dish for a get-away weekend or dinner by the fire. Autumn Soup with Cinnamon-Pepper Croutons turns the lowly yam into a savory, cold-weather soup flavored with fresh sage, rosemary, and thyme (and those sweet and zesty croutons are good enough to munch on their own).

As far as dinner goes, there's a reason writer and humorist Calvin Trillin wants to replace Thanksgiving turkey with Spaghetti alla Carbonara. It's the bacon, what else? Bacon makes Sunday night meat loaf irresistible and can wrap itself around a filet mignon better than a bow around a present, as you'll discover with Schmidty's Meat Loaf with Biscuits Instead and Bacon-Wrapped Filet Mignon with Maker's Mark Peppercorn Sauce. And for plain, old-fashioned comfort, Marvelous Mashed Potatoes with Bacon is a meal by itself. Speaking of vegetables, if you have kids, this book (and the bacon) will entice them to eat their leafy greens, beans, and even zucchini.

You might assume there's no dessert that could possibly taste better with bacon, but you're in for a surprise. The dessert recipes you'll find here will delight you. Your friends will rave about the Pear-Apple Crisp with Brown Sugar-Bacon Topping, the

**HAPPILY EVER AFTER**

In England, throughout the Middle Ages, if a man and wife could prove their first year of marriage was blissful and free of disharmony, they were entitled to a flitch, or slab, of bacon. From this custom came the saying "bringing home the bacon."

**IT'S TAX TIME! WHERE'S MY BLT?**

It's official. In the United States, April is National BLT Month. That's right, folks, but where are we gonna find a sun-ripened tomato in April?

Ruby Raisin Mincemeat Tart with Mulled Wine Sorbet, and the Try-It-You'll-Like-It Bacon Brittle (as the name suggests, one bite and the whole batch is history).

Cooks have always known that bacon adds shadowy richness, earthy fragrance, and subtle nuance to elegant entrées and everyday comfort foods such as baked beans, chowders, and pies. That's because bacon has two humble but charismatic ingredients that transform every food it touches: salt and fat. Salt brings out flavor, and fat carries flavor to our taste buds. But not only that—bacon has bite. It's chewy and crunchy. Savory. Slightly sweet. And habit-forming.

Like an artist who's had a career slump, bacon is enjoying a renaissance. It's about time. Previously disgraced as a fat, preservative-laden meat, bacon now offers many healthier options. It's leaner; it's tastier; it's free of chemicals, too. Artisan-style farms are raising pigs without hormones or antibiotics, and they're producing natural organic bacons that satisfy an appetite for old-fashioned flavor. You'll find them mentioned throughout this book, as well as information on where to find them (see Sources, page 128).

# WHAT IS BACON?

**BACON IS CURED PORK,** one of those wonderful creations that arose out of necessity. Before refrigeration, the only way to preserve meat was to cure it. In China, techniques for curing pork were developed nearly four thousand years ago. In Rome, sometime during the first century A.D., the epicurean nobleman Marcus Gavius Apicius wrote the world's first-known recipe book and naturally included a method for curing meat. In his book, he instructs cooks to salt the meat for 17 days, dry it for 2 days in the open air, and then smoke it for an additional 2 days. Little has changed in two thousand years, except that Apicius recommended storing the cured meat in oil and vinegar.

Salt dehydrates the meat and kills the microbes by dehydrating them, too. It also seems to change the color of the meat. This is not actually the result of the salt but of an impurity in the salt, a naturally occurring nitrate. During the Middle Ages, saltpeter (potassium nitrate) was discovered. Initially it was used as a fertilizer and in gunpowder, but made the leap to meat in the sixteenth or seventeenth century after it was learned that it had a positive effect on bacon's color and flavor when it was used in curing.

Right: **BRIE AND BACON FRITTATA,** see page 34

**BACON COMES IN MANY STRIPES**

This abbreviated list includes some of the more popular types.

**American-Style Bacon** traditionally comes from the pig's belly. It is salt-cured and wood-smoked, and the rind is removed before slicing.

**Boiling Bacon** is cured pork collar. It contains more fat than other cuts. Usually sold boned and rolled, it is the main ingredient in the Irish classic, boiled bacon and cabbage (forget corned beef!).

**Canadian Bacon** is cured pork loin with a flavor and texture similar to ham.

In the United States, bacon was a staple in the colonists' larder (the word *larder* comes from the Latin word for bacon fat). In the 1600s, early colonists used English recipes to cure bacon but soon learned new ones from the Indians who cured venison.

Today, with refrigeration, curing is done simply to add flavor to meat. We're accustomed to the cured taste, and we like it. But because dry salt-curing and smoking are time consuming and expensive, most large-scale meat processors cure their bacon in a salt brine, to which other flavorings and sweeteners are added, or inject their meats with a saline solution, using hundreds of needles to pump up weight (and profit margins). That's one reason why many bacons exude a whitish, watery fluid when cooked.

Because studies suggest nitrates are carcinogenic, many people are concerned about nitrates in bacon. The amount of nitrates has been steadily decreasing in all bacon, and it is now possible to obtain nitrate-free bacon. So, be sure to read label ingredients.

Small artisan-style bacon producers offer bacon lovers a new and growing market of delicious bacons that don't shrivel; they sizzle. There are a wonderful range of bacons from which to choose that are dry-cured or brine-cured in simple salt and sugar solutions, often without nitrates (see Sources, page 128).

While all bacon is cured, not all bacon is smoked. Smoking is done to give the cured meat a distinctive flavor or a particular taste, depending on the kind of hardwood and the process used. The most popular woods are hickory, apple, oak, and maple. (Soft, resinous evergreen wood is never selected because it imparts an undesirable flavor.) Typically, after the bacon is cured, the meat is dried. Then it is hung in a smokehouse with smoldering logs, chips, or sawdust for as little as several hours or as long as several weeks, ready to emerge and make our day. But be aware; with today's penchant for fast and cheap, the smoked flavor is not always a result of natural wood and fire. Out there lurks an inferior way, using injected smoked flavoring. Needless to say, it's something to avoid. Once again, be sure to read the label or ask your butcher.

Once you've bought the best bacon you can buy, take it home, cook it up, and take a big bite before you try any of the recipes in this book. You'll know then, if you didn't know before, why everything tastes better with bacon.

**Couenne** is the French term for bacon rind. Used to add flavor and a gelatinous texture to dishes, it is often put in the bottom of the stew pot to prevent other ingredients from sticking.

**Gammon** is a British term for bacon, smoked or not, made from the top of the pig's hind legs. It is cured while still part of the carcass. When the leg is removed from the carcass and then cured, it is known as ham.

**Green Bacon** is a term used to describe bacon that has been cured but not smoked.

**Hungarian Gypsy Bacon** is cured with spices and pig's blood before smoking. While it needs no cooking and can be served as a first course with other cured meats, it is also enjoyed sizzling hot and heavily sprinkled with paprika.

**Irish Bacon** is leaner than North American–style bacon. It is sometimes compared to Canadian bacon because of its meaty appearance.

# WHAT'S IN A SLICE, ANYWAY?

**WHETHER YOU ENJOY** it by the slice or parcel it out as a seasoning, you've probably wondered how fattening bacon is and whether it has any redeeming nutritional value. If you're among those who've been told bacon's taboo, here's the skinny.

Bacon is a source of protein (4%), and also contains vitamins, iron, zinc, copper, and selenium. Uncooked bacon is far higher in calories and fat than cooked bacon. One *cooked*, meat-streaked thick bacon slice (6.3 grams or a little more than .25 ounce) has 36 calories, is 6% fat, and has 101 milligrams sodium (4%). One *uncooked*, meat-streaked thick bacon slice (22.67 grams or a little less than 1 ounce) has 126 calories, is 24% fat, and has 155 milligrams sodium (6%).

Obviously, a lot of fat melts away during cooking. The values change depending on the leanness of your bacon. Remember, if you use uncooked bacon in a stew, soup, or other dish, the fat has not been removed in the cooking process.

**Lardon** is a thick, meaty bacon piece, about $1/4$ inch wide and 1 inch long. It refers to a thick, diced cube of slab bacon.

**Macon** is bacon made from mutton.

**Pancetta** is an Italian bacon that is cured or pickled but not smoked. It comes in a long, sausagelike roll.

**Pepper Bacon** is bacon, smoked or not, that is covered with a crust of ground black pepper. Often enjoyed at breakfast and in recipes calling for a peppery zing, it is readily available in supermarkets.

**Prosciutto** is the Italian word for ham. Cured and air-dried but not smoked, prosciutto is usually sold in paper-thin slices.

**Rasher** is the British word for a slice of bacon or ham.

# BRINGIN' HOME THE BACON

# BUYING BACON

**WITH A LITTLE KNOWLEDGE** and a sharp eye, you can find good bacon at your super-market as well as from the butcher, the deli, and the specialty-food shop. First, look at a whole slice. It should have an equal ratio of meat to fat. The bacon should be streaky, without large pockets of fat. Check out the fat, which should be ivory in color and firm and fine-textured to the touch. Depending on how the meat was cured, its color can range from pinkish-red to dark reddish-brown or mahogany. Since bacon varies from pig to pig, package to package, and slice to slice, it stands to reason that the leaner the bacon, the more the meat and the less the drippings.

A majority of presliced bacon is vacuum-packed in 1-pound packages, and the slices are usually presented shingle-style, one slice overlapping the next. Sliced bacon also comes prepackaged in stacks. With shingle-style bacon, it's fairly easy to count the number of slices per pound and divide to determine weight per slice. Remember, the fewer slices there are per pound, the thicker each slice will be.

If you have difficulty finding good bacon or want to try artisan-style bacons from different parts of the country, consider mail order and the Web (see Sources, page 128). With today's speedy delivery services, a Berkeley baconophile can order a corncob-smoked, thick-cut Kentucky bacon this morning and have it for dinner by the Bay tomorrow night. If you're wondering about cost, artisan-style bacon averages a little more than twice the cost of supermarket bacon.

# BACON TYPES

**THICK-SLICED BACON** is also known as "country style." Each slice is about $1/8$ inch thick. One pound (16 ounces) typically yields 12 to 16 slices. Many of the artisan-style or cottage-industry bacons are thick sliced.

**REGULAR-SLICED BACON** generally refers to vacuum-packed supermarket bacon. Each slice is about $1/16$ inch thick. One pound (16 ounces) typically yields 18 to 22 slices.

**THIN-SLICED BACON** is found in supermarkets and in restaurants where the meals are cheap, the delivery is fast, and the bacon disappears in a bite. It doesn't take long to cook up a $\frac{1}{32}$-inch-thick slice. One pound (16 ounces) typically yields 35 to 40 slices.

**SLAB BACON** is usually less expensive than sliced bacon and is available from most butchers and through mail-order (see Sources, page 128). It keeps longer than sliced bacon when refrigerated. Cut into slices as needed, slab bacon is popular with cooks who prefer very thick bacon slices, cubed bacon, or lardons.

**READY-TO-MICROWAVE BACON** is packaged in specially designed microwavable packets that absorb the drippings and are tossed after each use. No muss; no fuss; no fun; no way. If you're interested, read the package instructions.

**BACON ENDS AND PIECES** are used in recipes where uniform slices aren't necessary or desired, such as casseroles, soups, stews, and garnishes. They are less expensive to buy but just as flavorful.

# STORING BACON

## Refrigerating

**SLICED AND SLAB BACON:** Whether you purchase bacon vacuum-packed or buy it sliced and wrapped from a butcher shop or deli counter, refrigerate opened bacon in moisture-proof plastic wrap or sealable freezer bags. Store in the meat drawer or in the coldest part of your refrigerator (36° to 40°F) for up to 7 days. For longer storage, you'll need to freeze it. Slab bacon, which is cut into slices as needed, has less surface area exposed to the air and will keep for up to 6 weeks in the meat drawer or the coldest part of your refrigerator. As with sliced bacon, it should be carefully wrapped and sealed in moistureproof plastic wrap or sealable freezer bags.

**UNOPENED VACUUM-PACKED BACON:** Before buying or storing vacuum-packed bacon, check the "open by date" information on the package. Keep unopened packages in the meat drawer or in the coldest part of your refrigerator (36° to 40°F) for up to 3 weeks and use by their freshness date.

## Freezing

**BACON,** like any meat that is cured and smoked using salt, takes longer to freeze. Because this slower freezing affects the fat and flavor, sliced or slab bacon should not be frozen longer than 1 month.

**SLICED BACON:** To make it easy to get just the number of slices you need for a recipe or breakfast treat, line a baking sheet with waxed or parchment paper or the butcher paper used to wrap the bacon. Arrange the slices in parallel rows so they are not touching. Lay another piece of paper over the slices and continue. Place the baking sheet in the freezer for 2 to 3 hours. Once the slices are frozen solid, remove and repackage in moistureproof sealable freezer bags. The slices will be easy to stack and easy to remove, 1 slice at a time. Using an indelible pen, write the type of bacon and date of storage on the bags. Use within 1 month.

**UNOPENED VACUUM-PACKED BACON:** Wrap the package in moistureproof freezer wrap or in a sealable freezer bag and freeze for up to 1 month.

# COOKING GREAT BACON

## Stove-top Skillet

**FOR CRISP,** as-you-like-it bacon, nothing beats cooking it in a cold cast-iron skillet. It's also the best way to enjoy the delicious aroma. (Recall your first memory of bacon? Mine is that rise-and-shine smell of weekend bacon frying on the stove.) Bottom line: With a top-quality bacon, use a cold, heavy skillet; it's the only way.

For whole slices, let the bacon reach room temperature. In a cold, heavy skillet large enough to hold the slices in a single layer, arrange the slices and cook over low to medium-low heat. Does that seem too low? Are you used to hot bacon fat spitting at you? No more. Cooking bacon at a low temperature prevents shrinking, curling, and uneven cooking. It's time to say "So long!" to that roller-coaster bacon blackened on the crest and barely cooked on the downhill.

One of the pleasures of cooking bacon is turning the slices as often as you like and watching them brown to the desired crispness. When the bacon is cooked the way you like it, transfer the slices to paper towels to drain. In between batches, pour the drippings into a heatproof container.

**FYI:** One thick, 1-ounce bacon slice cooked over medium-low heat takes 10 to 12 minutes; 1 regular slice takes about 5 minutes.

**FOR BACON PIECES** and crumbled bacon, cut chilled bacon slices crosswise into 1-inch pieces and proceed as directed for whole slices. The smaller pieces allow you to cook more bacon, up to 10 ounces in a medium skillet. When cooking larger amounts, you may need to spoon out the drippings.

## Baking

**WHEN A LOT OF BACON IS NEEDED,** professionals often bake the slices with good results. Here are several techniques:

**PREHEAT** the oven to 350°F. To elevate the bacon slices, fill a rimmed baking sheet with crinkled aluminum foil or line it with wire racks. Or, use a broiler pan. Arrange the bacon slices in a single layer on the foil, the racks, or the broiler pan's slotted lid and bake to desired crispness, 15 to 20 minutes. It is not necessary to turn the slices.

**TRANSFER THE BACON** to paper towels to drain. While the slices look and taste good, their texture can be limp.

**ALTERNATELY,** arrange the bacon slices directly on the rimmed baking sheet and bake to desired crispness. Transfer the bacon to paper towels to drain. Because the slices are in direct contact with the drippings (as in a skillet), they are crisper than bacon raised above the drippings.

**IN A HURRY?** For faster cooking, arrange the bacon slices on a rimmed baking sheet using one of the previous methods. Then bake at 400°F for 10 to 15 minutes or at 500°F for 7 to 10 minutes. Transfer the bacon to paper towels to drain.

## Broiling

**PREHEAT** the broiler. Arrange the bacon slices in a single layer on the broiler pan's slotted lid. Place the oven rack so that the bacon slices are 3 inches from the heat source. Turn slices once for even browning and broil to desired crispness, 5 to 7 minutes. Watch carefully so the bacon doesn't burn. Transfer the bacon to paper towels to drain.

18

**TOOLS OF THE TRADE:** A *bacon press* or *iron* is a flat disk or plate used to weigh down bacon slices while they're cooking. It is designed to keep shrinkage to a minimum and create straight-as-an-arrow slices. A *spatter screen* is a fine-mesh screen that fits over the skillet to keep sputtering bacon fat from leaving the pan. If you choose high-quality bacon and cook at a low temperature, neither tool is really necessary.

## Microwaving

**OKAY,** so you're in a hurry, and you want your bacon *fast*. My own feeling is that microwaving bacon takes all the romance out of it. A turn of the dial and it's over, leaving you with bacon that's dry and hard. I guess people in a hurry can't always be romantic.

**ON A MICROWAVABLE PLATE,** sandwich 6 to 8 bacon slices between layers of paper towels. Cook on high for 6 to 8 minutes, checking the bacon every 2 minutes. For less fuss and fewer towels, special microwave bacon racks are available.

## Blanching

**FOR PEOPLE** who prefer more of a true pork flavor or who want to limit their salt intake, blanching or cooking bacon slices in boiling water will remove most of the salt as well as some of the fat and smoky flavor.

**IN A CAST-IRON SKILLET,** arrange the slices in a single layer. Cover the bacon with boiling water and simmer over low to medium-low heat for 2 to 3 minutes. Drain the water and continue to sauté the bacon to desired crispness.

## Handling

**WITH ANY RAW MEAT,** it is best to be cautious. Wash cutting boards, any utensils, and your hands with hot, soapy water after use. (Did you know that doctors and nurses are supposed to scrub their hands for a full 15 seconds to make sure they're clean?)

**IN THE PAST,** consumers worried about trichinosis in pork products. That concern is eliminated when bacon is cured or hot-smoked to USDA standards but, to be safe, it is wise not to taste or eat raw or uncooked bacon.

# WITHOUT BACON
# IT JUST
# AIN'T BREAKFAST

Rise-and-shine recipes for wakin' with bacon

# Two-Bite Bacon Biscuits with Homemade Apple Butter

Bits of scrumptious bacon make these flaky biscuits a hit at breakfast, especially when they're served with homemade apple butter. It's one of those I-can't-believe-it's-so-good combinations. Next thing you know, you'll crave them other times of the day, too. Go ahead, use this recipe for an easy hors d'oeuvre. For variation, add a sliver of cooked chicken, ham, or smoked salmon along with the apple butter.

**MAKES ABOUT 24 BISCUITS**

3     thick smoked bacon slices (3 ounces uncooked), cut crosswise into 1-inch pieces

2     cups all-purpose flour, plus more as needed

$1/2$     teaspoon salt

2     teaspoons baking powder

$1/2$     teaspoon baking soda

4     tablespoons cold unsalted butter, cut into pieces

$3/4$     cup buttermilk

Homemade Apple Butter (recipe follows)

**IN A MEDIUM HEAVY SKILLET,** cook the bacon pieces over low to medium-low heat, turning as needed to achieve uniform crispness. Using a slotted spoon, transfer to a paper towel to drain. Pour 2 tablespoons drippings into a shallow glass or metal container and freeze until hard, 20 to 30 minutes. Chop the bacon into fine bits. When the bacon drippings have hardened, remove and cut or break into pieces.

**PREHEAT** the oven to 450°F.

**IN A MEDIUM BOWL,** whisk together the flour, salt, baking powder, and baking soda. Add the butter and frozen drippings. Using a pastry blender, 2 knives, or your fingertips, work the mixture together until it is crumbly and resembles coarse meal. Stir in the bacon bits. Make a well in the center of the flour mixture. Pour the buttermilk into the well and stir until the mixture just forms a soft dough. Don't overbeat.

**DUST YOUR HANDS** with flour and knead the dough gently on a lightly floured surface 2 or 3 times. Roll out the dough to $1/2$ inch thick. Dip a 2-inch round cookie or biscuit cutter into the flour, shake off the excess, and push the cutter straight down to cut the dough. (If you twist the cutter, chances are the biscuits will not rise properly.) Place the biscuits about 1 inch apart on an ungreased baking sheet. Bake until lightly golden, about 10 minutes. Serve warm with apple butter.

# HOMEMADE APPLE BUTTER

**It's the essence of apples, and you'll find yourself eating this smooth and silky butter by the spoonful, over French vanilla ice cream, sandwiched between homemade molasses cookies, or with anything else that strikes your fancy.**

**MAKES ABOUT 1½ CUPS**

3    medium apples, peeled, cored, and
      chopped (see Note)
8    cups apple cider (not juice)
Sugar (optional)

**IN A 2- TO 3-QUART HEAVY SAUCEPAN,** combine the apples and 4 cups of the cider. Bring the mixture to a simmer over medium heat. Cook, stirring frequently, until the mixture is reduced and the apples resemble coarse applesauce, about 1 hour. Add the remaining 4 cups cider, 1 cup at a time, stirring occasionally, as the mixture thickens. The total cooking time will be 3 to 4 hours. During the last hour, reduce the heat to medium-low, stirring frequently to prevent the mixture from sticking to the pan and burning. Remove from heat and cool to room temperature. The apple butter will thicken as it cools. Taste and adjust sweetness by adding sugar, if needed. Store in a covered container in the refrigerator for up to 1 month.

**Note:** For apple butter, use more acidic apples, such as Bramley's Seedling, Cortland, Fuji, Grimes Golden, McIntosh, or Mutsu.

**EVERYTHING TASTES BETTER WITH BACON**

Variation:
# FOR CHUNKY HOMEMADE APPLE BUTTER,

follow the previous recipe, decreasing the total apple cider to about 5 cups and the cooking to 2 hours.

# Daddy's Fluffy Scrambled Eggs with Bacon

While there are faster ways to scramble eggs, Daddy knew that the sure way to make fluffy scrambled eggs was to cook them slowly in a double boiler with melted butter. Served with plenty of crisp pepper bacon, toasted and buttered French bread, and warm raspberry jam, this makes the best breakfast imaginable (supper, too).

Don't forget, to cook crisp bacon, have the bacon at room temperature and use a cold, heavy skillet over low to medium-low heat. You'll have time; the eggs take a while, and besides, it smells so good. For those mornings when there's something to celebrate, try James Beard's favorite way to cook bacon—with brown sugar.

**SERVES 2**

2    tablespoons unsalted butter
4    eggs
Coarse (kosher) salt and freshly ground pepper
4 to 6 thick pepper bacon slices
     (4 to 6 ounces uncooked)
4    French bread slices, toasted and buttered,
     for serving
Raspberry jam, warmed, for serving

**IN THE TOP PAN OF A DOUBLE BOILER** over simmering water, melt the butter.

**IN A MEDIUM BOWL,** briefly whisk together the eggs, about 10 seconds. Add a pinch of salt and a grinding of pepper to taste. Pour the egg mixture into the top of the double boiler and cook, stirring constantly with a wooden spoon, until the eggs form soft curds, about 8 minutes. Taste and adjust seasonings with salt and pepper.

**MEANWHILE,** in a medium heavy skillet, place the bacon slices in a single layer and cook over low to medium-low heat, turning as needed to achieve uniform crispness. Transfer to a paper towel to drain. Divide the eggs and the bacon between 2 warmed plates. Serve immediately with toasted and buttered French bread and warm jam.

## Variation:

### FOR JB'S BROWN SUGAR BACON,

cook the bacon as described above. When the bacon is beginning to brown, heavily sprinkle each slice with light or dark brown sugar and continue to cook until the sugar has melted, about 1 minute. Turn the slices and sprinkle with more sugar, if desired. Watch carefully so the bacon doesn't overbrown or the sugar over-caramelize. Drain on paper towels and serve.

# Never-a-Leftover Breakfast Bread Pudding

Bread pudding is a terrific way to use leftovers, but why not splurge? Buy the best ingredients you can find: crusty, porous Italian ciabatta olive bread, imported smoked Gouda cheese, roasted sweet red peppers—and the ultimate flavor ingredient, Nueske's applewood-smoked bacon. Lucky you, you'll get a triple hit. First, as the bacon fries (the aroma), then as the pudding bakes (there's that aroma again), and finally, as you tuck in and eat every bite.

As with most bread puddings, this one should be made at least 6 hours before baking to let the bread absorb the liquid and to let the flavors develop.

**SERVES 4 TO 6**

8  thick Nueske's or other artisan-style applewood-smoked bacon slices (8 ounces uncooked), cut crosswise into 1-inch pieces (see Sources, page 128)

6  eggs

2  cups half-and-half

1  tablespoon Dijon mustard

1/4  teaspoon coarse (kosher) salt

1/2  teaspoon freshly ground pepper

1  loaf (15 ounces) ciabatta olive bread, cut into 12 to 15 slices and slightly stale (see Note)

1 1/4  cups (about 5 ounces) grated smoked Gouda cheese

1/2  cup julienned jarred roasted sweet red peppers

**SPRAY OR BUTTER** a 9-by-9-by-2 1/2-inch baking pan.

**IN A MEDIUM HEAVY SKILLET,** cook the bacon pieces over low to medium-low heat, turning as needed to brown but not crisp. Using a slotted spoon, transfer to a paper towel to drain.

**IN A MEDIUM BOWL,** whisk together the eggs, half-and-half, mustard, salt, and pepper until blended.

**ARRANGE** half of the bread slices in the bottom of the prepared pan and top with half of the cheese, three-fourths of the bacon, and three-fourths of the red peppers. Arrange the remaining bread slices over the first layer. Top with the remaining cheese, bacon, and peppers. Carefully pour the egg mixture over the bread and, with the back of a spatula, lightly press the assembled pudding. Cover loosely with aluminum foil and refrigerate for at least 6 hours, preferably overnight.

**PREHEAT** the oven to 375°F.

**BAKE THE PUDDING,** covered, for 35 minutes. Remove the foil, reduce the temperature to 275°F, and bake until golden brown, 15 to 20 minutes. Let sit for 15 minutes before serving.

 **Note:** To make fresh bread slightly stale, arrange the slices on a wire rack and let sit at room temperature overnight, or dry the slices in a preheated 200°F oven for 20 minutes.

# Hangtown Fry

In 1849, a Northern California prospector struck it rich on the banks of Hangtown Creek, right in the middle of town. Hungry for praise and a good meal, the fortunate fellow headed for the saloon and ordered the priciest dishes on the menu. Those items turned out to be bacon, eggs, and oysters. The bacon came by ship from around Cape Horn; the eggs, by carriage over a rough Hangtown road; and the oysters, by stagecoach from San Francisco's bay. Instead of asking for separate plates, the miner told the cook to combine them. Eureka!

## SERVES 2

4  thick smoked or pepper bacon slices (4 ounces uncooked), cut crosswise into 1-inch pieces
4  tablespoons crushed soda crackers
3  tablespoons all-purpose flour
Coarse (kosher) salt and freshly ground pepper
4 to 6 fresh raw oysters, shucked, drained, and patted dry
4  eggs
Pinch of cayenne pepper
1  tablespoon half-and-half or heavy (whipping) cream
1  tablespoon unsalted butter
1  tablespoon chopped fresh flat-leaf parsley
4  sourdough bread slices, toasted and buttered, for serving
2  tablespoons finely chopped shallots or onion (optional)
$^1/_3$  cup rice wine vinegar (optional)

**IN A MEDIUM HEAVY SKILLET,** cook the bacon pieces over low to medium-low heat, turning as needed to achieve uniform crispness. Using a slotted spoon, transfer to a paper towel to drain. Pour off the bacon drippings, reserving 1 tablespoon in the skillet. Crumble the bacon and set aside.

**IN A SMALL BOWL,** mix together the soda crackers, flour, and salt and pepper to taste. Lightly coat the oysters and set aside.

**IN A MEDIUM BOWL,** whisk together the eggs, cayenne pepper, and half-and-half until blended and set aside.

**IN THE SAME SKILLET** used to cook the bacon, heat the reserved drippings and butter over medium heat. Add the oysters and sauté for 1 minute per side. Pour the egg mixture over the oysters and reduce the heat to medium-low. Cook until the edges are set, $1^1/_2$ to 2 minutes. With a spatula, lift the edge in several places and tip the skillet so the uncooked egg in the center runs underneath. When the surface is moist and no liquid remains, sprinkle the crumbled bacon over the top. Cover and cook until the eggs are set, 3 to 5 minutes. Slide onto a platter, garnish with parsley, and serve with the toasted and buttered sourdough bread.

**IF DESIRED,** in a small serving bowl, mix together the shallots and rice wine vinegar and set aside. At the table, drizzle the shallot and rice wine vinegar over the eggs.

# Sweetie-Pie Pancake with Brown Sugar Apples and Bacon

The batter is light and eggy; the apples, deliciously tart. And the bacon? Salty, savory, and sublime. Add the sweetness of brown sugar (and your own sweetie pie), and this high-rising pancake has everything you want. Just be sure to serve immediately because like a soufflé, it will deflate.

**SERVES 2 TO 4**

3    eggs at room temperature

$1/2$    cup milk at room temperature

Pinch of salt

$1/2$    cup all-purpose flour

3    thick smoked or unsmoked bacon slices (3 ounces uncooked), cut crosswise into $1/2$-inch pieces

1    medium or 2 small crisp, tart apples

2    tablespoons unsalted butter

$1/4$    cup firmly packed dark brown sugar

Powdered sugar for dusting

**PREHEAT** the oven to 425°F.

**IN A MEDIUM BOWL,** whisk together the eggs, milk, salt, and flour until combined. The batter may be slightly lumpy. Set aside.

**IN AN OVENPROOF MEDIUM HEAVY SKILLET,** cook the bacon pieces over low to medium-low heat, turning as needed to brown but not crisp. Using a slotted spoon, transfer to a paper towel to drain. Pour off the bacon drippings.

**PEEL, CORE, AND CUT** the apples into $1/4$-inch slices. In the same skillet, melt the butter over medium heat. Add the apple slices and sauté for 3 minutes. Turn the apples and sauté for 3 minutes longer. (If you're Type A, like me, feel free to arrange the slices in a circular tartlike pattern.) Sprinkle the apples with the brown sugar, then with the bacon. Cook for 1 minute.

**WHISK THE BATTER** for 30 seconds and pour it over the apple mixture. Bake until the pancake puffs up and is golden brown, about 15 minutes. Using an oven mitt to hold the skillet's hot handle, remove from the oven. Dust the pancake with powdered sugar, slice, and serve immediately.

# Sergeant Preston's Fried-Egg Sandwich

**Sustained only by fried-egg sandwiches chock-full of bacon and wrapped in hide for easy eating, radio good-guy Sergeant Preston and his husky, Yukon King, captured bad guys, survived avalanches, and crossed the frozen North. Me, I wrap my fried-egg sandwich deli-style in a paper towel.**

**SERVES 1**

2    thick bacon slices (2 ounces uncooked),
      cut crosswise in half
1    small potato, cut into $1/4$-inch dice (about $1/3$ cup)
1    egg
Coarse (kosher) salt and freshly ground pepper
2    sourdough bread slices

**IN A SMALL HEAVY SKILLET,** place the bacon slices in a single layer and cook over low to medium-low heat for 3 minutes. Add the diced potato and cook, turning often, until the bacon is crisp and the potato is golden brown, 7 to 8 minutes. Transfer the potato and the bacon to a paper towel to drain, leaving the skillet on the heat and as much of the drippings behind as possible.

**BREAK THE EGG** into the skillet and season with salt and pepper to taste. Cook over medium-low to medium heat, sunny-side up, until the white is set but the yolk is still runny, about 4 minutes. Using a spatula, gently remove the fried egg and set aside.

**PLACE THE BREAD SLICES** in the skillet and fry until toasted on one side, about 1 minute.

**TO ASSEMBLE,** place one bread slice, toasted-side down, on a plate. Place the bacon slices on it, then the egg. With a knife, break the yolk and spread it across the white. Sprinkle the potatoes over the egg and top with the other bread slice, toasted-side up.

**TO SERVE ON THE RUN,** wrap the sandwich deli-style in a paper towel, butcher paper, or parchment paper. To eat at the table, serve on a plate with a knife and fork.

# Bacon Quiche

Let's bring back the quiche. After all, it's been a classic bacon-and-egg dish since the sixteenth century. Back then, in Lorraine, a region in northeastern France, it was served on May Day as a celebration dish alongside roast suckling pig. When Julia Child introduced the quiche to television viewers in the '70s, the American audience went hog-wild (until the "real men" phenomenon). It's time to return to the golden days.

I adore this savory tart because of its marvelous contrasts: the flaky crust, the creamy egg custard, and the crisp, salty bacon—especially the bacon. An unsmoked one is best so it doesn't overpower the other ingredients. Hempler's Meat & Sausages bacon, made in Washington state, is a good choice (see Sources, page 128, under The Grateful Palate).

If you're like me and you hesitate when a crust is involved, you can always opt for the easy way out. Keep some ready-made dough or prebaked pie crusts from the supermarket in your freezer. There are some good ones out there. As a last resort, you can skip the crust altogether, but be sure to bake the crustless quiche in a Pyrex pie plate so your quiche doesn't leak or weep.

**SERVES 6**

**CRUST:**

1 1/2 cups all-purpose flour

1/4 teaspoon salt

5 tablespoons cold unsalted butter, cut into pieces

2 tablespoons cold shortening, cut into pieces

4 to 6 tablespoons ice water

**FILLING:**

6 thick unsmoked bacon slices (6 ounces uncooked), cut crosswise into 1-inch pieces

3/4 cup minced shallots

1/2 teaspoon sugar

3 eggs

1 1/4 cups half-and-half

Large pinch of nutmeg

Coarse (kosher) salt and freshly ground pepper

1/2 cup (2 ounces) grated Swiss Gruyère cheese

**TO MAKE THE CRUST:** In a medium bowl, whisk together the flour and salt. Add the butter and shortening. Using a pastry blender, 2 knives, or your fingertips, work the mixture together until it is crumbly and resembles coarse meal. Sprinkle in the ice water, beginning with 4 tablespoons, and mix until the dough holds together when pressed. Shape into a disk, wrap in plastic wrap, and chill for 2 hours.

**PREHEAT** the oven to 375°F. Set aside a baking sheet. If desired, line with parchment paper for easy cleanup in case any filling overflows.

**LET THE DOUGH SOFTEN** slightly at room temperature. Place the dough on a lightly floured surface and roll it into a 10-inch circle. Ease the pastry into a 9-by-1-inch quiche pan with a removable bottom, fitting it against the bottom and sides. Chill 30 minutes to 1 hour. Prick the bottom of the crust with a fork, line with aluminum foil, and fill to the top with pie weights or dried beans. Bake in the center of the oven until the edges begin to turn golden, about 15 minutes. Remove the weights and foil and bake until golden, 8 to 10 minutes. Remove from the oven and let cool.

**TO MAKE THE FILLING:** In a medium heavy skillet, cook the bacon pieces over low to medium-low heat, turning as needed to brown but not crisp. Using a slotted spoon, transfer to a paper towel to drain. Pour off the bacon drippings, reserving 1 tablespoon in the skillet. Add the shallots and sauté over medium heat for 3 minutes. Sprinkle in the sugar and cook until the shallots are golden, about 1 minute. Set aside.

**IN A MEDIUM BOWL,** whisk together the eggs and half-and-half until blended. Stir in the nutmeg and salt and pepper to taste.

**PLACE THE TART PAN** on the baking sheet. Sprinkle the bottom of the crust with the shallots, then with the bacon and the cheese. Pour the egg mixture into the crust (it will reach the brim). Carefully place it in the oven, and bake until the top is puffed and golden and the eggs are set, about 35 minutes. Cool slightly before removing the quiche from the pan. Serve warm or at room temperature.

# Brie and Bacon Frittata

This Italian egg dish doesn't require a fancy flip or even an omelet pan. The eggs are lightly whisked and slowly cooked in a skillet until set. On top of the eggs, the creamy brie softly melts over the crumbled bacon, creating a dressed-up variation on the easy-going frittata. Tiny apple wedges, sprinkled in with the bacon, add just the right amount of sweetness.

### SERVES 2 TO 4

| | |
|---|---|
| 4 | thick bacon slices (4 ounces uncooked), cut crosswise into 1-inch pieces |
| 4 | eggs |
| $1/4$ | cup milk |
| 2 | tablespoons finely chopped fresh chives |
| $1/2$ | teaspoon coarse (kosher) salt |
| $1/4$ | teaspoon freshly ground pepper |
| $1/2$ | small red apple, such as Gala or Fuji |
| 1 | tablespoon unsalted butter |
| 2 | ounce piece of chilled Brie, rind removed, cut into small pieces |

**IN A MEDIUM HEAVY SKILLET,** cook the bacon pieces over low to medium-low heat, turning as needed to brown but not crisp. Using a slotted spoon, transfer to a paper towel to drain. Crumble the bacon and set aside.

**IN A MEDIUM BOWL,** whisk together the eggs, milk, chives, salt, and pepper until blended. Peel, core, and cut the apples into $1/8$-inch slices. Cut each slice into small bite-sized wedges and set aside.

**IN A MEDIUM NONSTICK SKILLET** with sloping sides, melt the butter over medium heat. When it begins to foam, add the egg mixture and reduce the heat to medium-low. Cook until the edges are set, $1^{1}/2$ to 2 minutes. With a spatula, lift the edge in several places and tip the skillet so the uncooked egg in the center runs underneath. When the surface is more moist than shiny and no liquid remains, sprinkle the crumbled bacon, apple, and Brie over the top. Cover and cook until the eggs are set and the cheese is melted, about 4 minutes. Remove from heat and let the fritatta sit, uncovered, for 1 minute. Cut into wedges and serve.

34

# Bacon and Eggs Rancheros

This zesty baked-egg dish is just the ticket to feeling indulged when you're cooking for one. What's even better is that it goes together quickly. Eggs rancheros usually call for chorizo sausage, but pepper bacon packs a lot of zing, especially when it's combined with a great-tasting, store-bought salsa like Rick Bayless's Frontera tomatillo or jalapeño cilantro salsa. By the way, when you're cooking for more than one, these ingredients multiply easily. Just use a larger skillet.

**SERVES 1**

2　thick pepper bacon slices (2 ounces uncooked), cut crosswise into 1-inch pieces

$1/2$　cup salsa, store-bought or homemade

2　eggs

$1/4$　cup (1 ounce) grated Jack or Cheddar cheese or a combination

Sour cream for garnishing

2　teaspoons coarsely chopped fresh cilantro, flat-leaf parsley, or basil

Coarse (kosher) salt and freshly ground pepper

Warm tortillas for serving

**IN A SMALL HEAVY SKILLET,** cook the bacon pieces over low to medium-low heat, turning as needed to achieve uniform crispness. Using a slotted spoon, transfer to a paper towel to drain. Pour off the bacon drippings, leaving enough to coat the skillet.

**WITH THE SKILLET OFF THE HEAT,** add the salsa and make 2 indentations. (Since salsas vary in thickness, don't be concerned if the indentations are somewhat runny. If the salsa is watery, consider straining it first.) Carefully break an egg into each indentation and set the skillet over medium heat. Cover and cook until the whites are almost set, about 5 minutes. Sprinkle on the cheese, then the bacon, and cover. Cook until the cheese has melted, about 1 minute. Slide the eggs and sauce onto a plate, and garnish with sour cream and cilantro. At the table, season with salt and pepper to taste. Serve with warm tortillas.

# FRESH GREENS
# AND CRISPY THINGS

Bacon is salad's best-kept secret

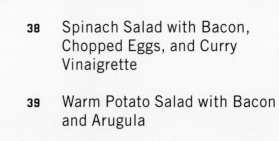

# Spinach Salad with Bacon, Chopped Eggs, and Curry Vinaigrette

**While this salad makes a great companion to grilled meats and roasted chicken, it also doubles as an entrée. Consider adding a lazy Susan filled with small bowls of curry-style toppings, such as golden raisins, dried cranberries, chopped roasted hazelnuts, peeled and seeded tomato chunks, finely sliced scallions, and slivered jalapeños. Diners will garnish with zest.**

**SERVES 4**

$^1/_3$   cup olive oil

$^1/_4$   cup white wine or champagne vinegar

$1^1/_2$ teaspoons soy sauce

1    teaspoon sugar

$^1/_2$   teaspoon dry mustard

$^1/_2$ to $^3/_4$ teaspoon curry powder

$^1/_4$   teaspoon garlic salt

$^1/_4$   teaspoon freshly ground pepper

5    thick bacon slices (5 ounces uncooked), cut crosswise into $^1/_2$-inch pieces

4    quarts (about 2 bunches) young spinach leaves, well rinsed and dried

2    hard-cooked eggs, chopped

**IN A SMALL BOWL,** whisk together the olive oil, vinegar, soy sauce, sugar, mustard, curry powder, garlic salt, and pepper. Set aside for 30 minutes, then adjust seasonings with curry powder to taste.

**IN A MEDIUM HEAVY SKILLET,** cook the bacon pieces over low to medium-low heat, turning as needed to achieve uniform crispness. Using a slotted spoon, transfer to a paper towel to drain.

**IN A LARGE SALAD BOWL,** gently toss the spinach and chopped eggs. Add the bacon. Pour half of the vinaigrette over the salad and toss to mix. Taste, adding additional vinaigrette if needed. Serve immediately.

# Warm Potato Salad with Bacon and Arugula

Still-warm baby new potatoes, smoky bacon bits, and a fresh herb vinaigrette combine their great tastes in this simple, earthy salad. A last-minute toss with fresh arugula adds a peppery bite and bright color. While this salad is delicious warm, it also can be served at room temperature and is a perfect match for grilled chicken or steak.

For a little more excitement, toss in a bit of crumbled Gorgonzola along with the arugula. You can add toasted walnuts, hazelnuts, or pecans, too. If you want a creamier dressing, try the Lemon-Caper Mayonnaise (see page 86). For an unusual entrée, cook your favorite pasta, toss it until just glossy with olive oil, then top it with this warm potato salad, and get ready for a feast.

**SERVES 4**

**VINAIGRETTE:**

$1/3$   cup olive oil

$1/4$   cup champagne vinegar

$1/2$   teaspoon Dijon mustard

2    cloves garlic, pressed

$1/2$   teaspoon coarse (kosher) salt

$1/2$   teaspoon medium-ground pepper

**SALAD:**

$1^{1}/2$ pounds golf ball–sized new potatoes

4 to 6 thick smoked or unsmoked bacon slices (4 to 6 ounces uncooked), cut crosswise into $3/4$-inch pieces

2    cups loosely packed trimmed tender, young arugula leaves

Coarse (kosher) salt and freshly ground pepper

**TO MAKE THE VINAIGRETTE:** In a salad bowl, whisk together the olive oil, vinegar, mustard, garlic, salt, and pepper.

**TO MAKE THE SALAD:** In a medium saucepan, cover the potatoes with cold, salted water. Partially cover the pan and cook over medium-high heat until tender, 15 to 20 minutes.

**MEANWHILE,** in a medium heavy skillet, cook the bacon pieces over low to medium-low heat, turning as needed to achieve uniform crispness. Using a slotted spoon, transfer to a paper towel to drain.

**DRAIN THE POTATOES** in a colander. When the potatoes are cool to the touch, cut them in half and add them to the salad bowl. Add the bacon pieces and toss with three-fourths of the vinaigrette. Just before serving, add the arugula, toss, and adjust the seasonings with salt, pepper, and dressing to taste.

**IF DESIRED,** the salad can be made 2 to 3 hours before serving and kept at room temperature or chilled.

39

# "*Mangia!*" Summer Bread Salad

Let's eat! This knife-and-fork salad, layered to look like an open-faced sandwich gone wild, comes from northern Italy. With a chilled bottle of Pinot Grigio, it makes a wonderful luncheon entrée. The red wine vinaigrette baptizes slices of country bread that are then topped with layers of crisp bacon, garden greens, and slices of ripe summer tomatoes, yellow pepper, fennel, and cucumber. For the best flavor, prepare the salad 1 hour before you plan on serving it.

**SERVES 4**

1    small clove garlic, pressed
1/2    cup extra-virgin olive oil
1/4    cup red wine vinegar
1/4    cup water
6    ciabatta or rustic-style bread slices, each 1/2 inch thick, slightly stale (see Note)
3    ripe medium tomatoes, thinly sliced
1    yellow bell pepper, seeded, deribbed, and thinly sliced
1/2    small fennel bulb, quartered, cored, and cut crosswise into paper-thin slices
1/2    cucumber, peeled and thinly sliced
4    large loose-leaf lettuce leaves, torn or sliced into strips
1/2    cup fresh basil leaves, torn into strips

6    crisply cooked thick bacon slices (6 ounces uncooked), cut crosswise into bite-sized pieces
Whole basil leaves for garnishing (optional)
3/4    cup shaved Parmigiano-Reggiano cheese (from a 1 1/2-ounce chunk) (optional)
Coarse (kosher) salt and freshly ground pepper

**IN A CUP OR SMALL BOWL,** mix together the garlic and olive oil and set aside.

**IN A CUP OR SMALL BOWL,** whisk together the vinegar and water. On a round serving platter, lay 2 bread slices side by side and lay another slice above, in a triangular pattern, so all the slices are touching. Drizzle the bread with half of the vinegar water.

**TOP WITH HALF OF THE TOMATOES,** bell pepper, fennel, cucumber, lettuce, basil, and bacon. Drizzle with half of the olive oil mixture. Repeat to make a second layer. Let sit for 1 hour. Just before serving, garnish with whole basil leaves and cheese, if desired. At the table, season with salt and pepper to taste.

 **Note:** To make fresh bread slightly stale, arrange the slices on a wire rack and let sit at room temperature overnight, or dry the slices in a preheated 200°F oven for 20 minutes.

# Pear Salad with Bacon and Honey-Hazelnut Vinaigrette

Fresh sweet pears and Roquefort have always been a winning combination. Here, the subtle flavor of hazelnuts and honey provides a bright, refreshing accent. Add a tasty bacon and you lift this salad to yet another dimension. When you're serving family, toss all the ingredients together. For a dinner party, compose the salad beautifully on separate plates and drizzle with the dressing.

In Oregon, where I live, Carlton produces a dry-cured bacon that is sweet and lean. It's a good one to use in this salad. For something with a bit of zing from Tennessee, try Tripp Country Ham bacon, brown-sugar cured with red pepper and cinnamon (see Sources, page 128, under The Grateful Palate).

| | |
|---|---|
| 2 | tablespoons hazelnut oil |
| 1 | teaspoon honey |
| $^1/_2$ | teaspoon Dijon mustard |
| $^1/_4$ | teaspoon coarse (kosher) salt |

Pinch of freshly ground pepper

| | |
|---|---|
| 1 | tablespoon rice wine vinegar |
| 2 | ripe but firm Bartlett pears, peeled, cored, and cut into 1-inch pieces |
| 4 | crisply cooked thick smoked or unsmoked bacon slices (4 ounces uncooked), cut crosswise into $^1/_2$-inch pieces |
| 1 | small head endive, sliced crosswise into 1-inch pieces |
| 2 | cups loosely packed trimmed tender, young arugula leaves |
| 1 | ounce Roquefort cheese, or best blue cheese available, crumbled |

**IN A SMALL CERAMIC OR GLASS BOWL,** mix together the oil and honey. (If the honey is thick, warm the mixture for a few seconds—no longer—in the microwave.) Whisk in the mustard, salt, pepper, and vinegar.

**IN A MEDIUM BOWL,** gently toss together the pears, bacon, endive, and arugula, lifting and blending the ingredients. Pour the vinaigrette over the salad, toss again, and divide among 4 chilled salad plates. Garnish each salad with crumbled cheese and serve immediately.

# Wild Greens with Apples and Warm Bacon Dressing

Here is a rendition of the quintessential French springtime salad made with crisp wild greens, sautéed apples, and a warm bacon dressing. Use a good, strong, smoky bacon. It makes all the difference.

In France, the classic preparation calls for slab bacon cut into 1/2-inch-thick lardons (see page 13). Check with your meat market to find out if your butcher carries slab bacon, or see Sources (page 128) for online and mail-order bacon suppliers who offer slab bacon. However, this recipe also works very well with thick bacon slices.

**SERVES 4**

8    thick smoked bacon slices (8 ounces uncooked), cut crosswise into 1-inch pieces
3    tablespoons cider vinegar
1    teaspoon Worcestershire sauce
1    teaspoon Dijon mustard
2    tablespoons firmly packed light brown sugar
1    medium red apple, such as Braeburn, Fuji, or Jonathan, cored and sliced into 16 thin, lengthwise slices

8    cups (about 7 ounces) loosely packed mixed tender, young bitter greens, such as dandelion, escarole, kale, mustard, and arugula
Coarse (kosher) salt and freshly ground pepper

**IN A MEDIUM HEAVY SKILLET,** cook the bacon pieces over low to medium-low heat, turning as needed to achieve uniform crispness. Using a slotted spoon, transfer to a paper towel to drain. Pour off the bacon drippings, reserving 3 tablespoons in the skillet.

**IN A SMALL BOWL,** whisk together the vinegar, Worcestershire sauce, mustard, and brown sugar.

**IN THE SKILLET** used to cook the bacon, add the vinegar mixture to the reserved bacon drippings. Warm over medium heat, using a wooden spoon to scrape up any browned bits stuck to the bottom of the skillet. (*Note:* When vinegar is heated, it creates steam, which can be irritating to the eyes.) Add the apple and sauté briefly until tender-crisp, about 1 minute.

**PUT THE GREENS** and the bacon pieces in a warmed salad bowl. Pour the warm dressing and apples over the greens. Toss the salad, taste, and season with salt and pepper, if needed. The saltiness of the bacon is often enough seasoning. Serve immediately.

43

# Cobb Salad

Some say actor Douglas Fairbanks Jr., created it—that late one night at Hollywood's Brown Derby Restaurant, the hungry screen idol and the restaurant's owner, Bob Cobb, raided the kitchen and tossed together a salad of leftovers.

Cobb's widow had a different story. She said that, after a difficult session with the dentist, Mr. Cobb went to work hungry and irritable. He asked the restaurant's chef to fix something he could eat. The chef looked around for ingredients he knew his boss would like and chopped them up as a salad. In either version, a star was born.

In the original, the dressing was a red wine vinaigrette. This rendition is tossed with a creamy tarragon-caper dressing that gives the whole creation a tangy, fresh taste.

**SERVES 4**

**DRESSING:**

½ cup mayonnaise

¼ cup sour cream

1 tablespoon tarragon or white wine vinegar

1 teaspoon fresh lemon juice

½ teaspoon anchovy paste

1 tablespoon finely chopped fresh flat-leaf parsley

1 tablespoon minced capers

1 green onion, both white and green parts, chopped to yield 1 tablespoon, or 1 tablespoon minced chives

1 teaspoon dried tarragon

Coarse (kosher) salt and freshly ground pepper

**SALAD:**

3 to 4 cups finely chopped inner leaves of romaine lettuce

4 to 6 crisply cooked thick bacon slices (4 to 6 ounces uncooked), cut crosswise into ¼-inch pieces

½ pound chicken breasts, cooked and cut into ¼-inch dice

1 large tomato, seeded and cut into ¼-inch dice

1 medium avocado, cut into ¼-inch dice

2 green onions, both white and green parts, chopped

1 or 2 hard-cooked eggs, cut into ¼-inch dice

2 ounces Roquefort cheese, or best blue cheese available, crumbled

**TO MAKE THE DRESSING:** The dressing is best if made several hours ahead or the day before. In a bowl, whisk together the mayonnaise, sour cream, vinegar, lemon juice, and anchovy paste. Stir in the parsley, capers, green onion, and tarragon. Season with salt and pepper to taste. Refrigerate in a covered container until ready to serve.

**TO MAKE THE SALAD:** In a large salad bowl, gently toss together the romaine, bacon, chicken, tomato, avocado, green onions, eggs, and cheese, lifting and blending the ingredients. Pour one-half of the dressing over the salad and toss to blend. Taste, adding additional dressing if needed. Serve immediately.

45

# Crunchy Bacon Coleslaw with Two (Okay, Three) Dressings

Coleslaws are popular in my family. When there's a picnic in the making or when salad greens are out of season (or too expensive), we go for something colorful and crunchy. Our slaws used to be mono-chromatic affairs—pale green cabbage with a mayo-celery seed dressing. Then, years ago, one of us must have read a *Bon Appétit* magazine because a colorful confetti of raw vegetables joined the slaw repertoire. About the same time, bacon starting showing up, first in bits as a gar-nish, then flavoring the whole salad.

Dressings seem to come and go with the sea-sons. Many in my family still favor the celery seed dressing. Others, like me, prefer the horseradish version. It has just the right bite. And, for a light and tangy dressing, out goes the mayonnaise and in comes a zesty tangerine vinaigrette. With those choices, you're bound to find a favorite.

**SERVES 4**

**DILL-HORSERADISH DRESSING:**

$1/2$ cup heavy (whipping) cream

$1/4$ cup mayonnaise

2 tablespoons prepared horseradish

$1/4$ teaspoon white pepper, plus more to taste

$1/2$ teaspoon firmly packed dark brown sugar

1 tablespoon fresh dill or 1 teaspoon dried

1 teaspoon rice wine vinegar

Coarse (kosher) salt

**SALAD:**

8 thick bacon slices (8 ounces uncooked), cut crosswise into $1/2$-inch pieces

1 small red apple, cored and cut into $1/2$-inch cubes

Juice of $1/2$ lemon

1 small yellow bell pepper, seeded and deribbed

1 small red bell pepper, seeded and deribbed

1 cup shredded red cabbage

1 cup shredded green cabbage

1 medium carrot, peeled and grated

3 or 4 green onions, both white and green parts, thinly sliced

46

**TO MAKE THE DRESSING:** In a medium bowl, whisk the cream until stiff peaks form. In another medium bowl, whisk together the mayonnaise, horseradish, white pepper, brown sugar, dill, and vinegar until blended. Add one-fourth of the whipped cream to the mayonnaise mixture and stir to blend. Then add the remaining whipped cream and gently fold until thoroughly combined. Taste and adjust seasonings with salt and white pepper. Cover and refrigerate until ready to use.

**TO MAKE THE SALAD:** In a medium heavy skillet, cook the bacon pieces over low to medium-low heat, turning as needed to achieve uniform crispness. Using a slotted spoon, transfer to a paper towel to drain. Coarsely chop three-fourths of the bacon; crumble the remaining and set aside.

**IN A SALAD BOWL,** toss the apple with the lemon juice. Cut the yellow and red bell peppers into $1/4$-inch strips, then cut the strips into $1/8$-inch diagonal slivers and add to the bowl. Add the red and green cabbage, carrot, and green onions. Toss with three-fourths of the dressing. Add the coarsely chopped bacon and toss.

**COVER AND REFRIGERATE** for 1 to 2 hours. Toss, taste, and add additional dressing, if needed. Garnish with the crumbled bacon and serve.

# ZESTY TANGERINE VINAIGRETTE

**IN A SMALL BOWL,** whisk together $1/3$ cup fresh tangerine juice, 1 teaspoon grated tangerine zest, 2 tablespoons rice wine vinegar, and 3 tablespoons canola or vegetable oil until blended. Whisk in coarse (kosher) salt and a pinch of cayenne pepper. Taste and adjust seasonings, adding 1 to 2 tablespoons tangerine juice, if desired.

# CELERY SEED DRESSING

**IN A SMALL BOWL,** whisk together $1/4$ cup sour cream, $1/4$ cup mayonnaise, 2 teaspoons cider vinegar, 2 teaspoons sugar, and 1 teaspoon celery seeds until blended. Whisk in coarse (kosher) salt and a pinch of freshly ground black pepper or cayenne pepper to taste.

# PASTA, POLENTA, AND RISOTTO WITH BACON

Italian cooking goes hog-wild

# Sizzling Herb Pasta with White Beans and Crisp Smoked Bacon

The combination of beans and pasta has always been one of Italy's great comfort foods. In this recipe, you marinate white beans in a lemony vinaigrette, cook smoked bacon until crisp, then sizzle garden-fresh herbs in the drippings. Toss them with fusilli, a spiral-shaped pasta, and serve an unbeatable 30-minute dish to family or company.

## SERVES 4

Zest of 1 large lemon, grated or minced

1   large clove garlic, pressed

1   tablespoon fresh lemon juice

1   tablespoon olive oil

1   can (15 ounces) white beans, drained and rinsed (about 1 1/2 cups)

4 to 6 thick smoked bacon slices (4 to 6 ounces uncooked), cut crosswise into 1- to 2-inch pieces

12 to 14 ounces dried fusilli

1 1/2 cups coarsely chopped fresh flat-leaf parsley

1/4   cup coarsely chopped fresh sage

2 to 3 tablespoons coarsely chopped fresh rosemary

Coarse (kosher) salt and freshly ground pepper

Grated Romano cheese for serving

**IN A SMALL BOWL,** whisk together the lemon zest, garlic, lemon juice, and olive oil. Stir in the beans and set aside.

**IN A MEDIUM HEAVY SKILLET,** cook the bacon pieces over low to medium-low heat, turning as needed to achieve uniform crispness. Using a slotted spoon, transfer to a paper towel to drain. Pour off the bacon drippings, reserving 1/4 cup in the skillet.

**MEANWHILE,** prepare the pasta according to package directions. Using plenty of boiling salted water, cook the pasta until al dente (tender but firm to the bite). (Serving hint: As the pasta water heats, place your serving bowl or platter over the pot to warm it.) Drain well, reserving 1/2 cup cooking water.

**TRANSFER THE PASTA** to the warmed serving bowl, add the beans with their marinade and the bacon pieces, and lightly toss.

**IN THE SKILLET** used to cook the bacon, heat the reserved bacon drippings over medium-high heat until hot. (To test, add an herb leaf to the hot drippings. When it sizzles, the temperature is right.) Add the parsley, sage, and rosemary to the hot drippings and sauté quickly, 10 to 15 seconds. Drizzle and scrape the bacon drippings and herbs onto the pasta mixture and toss to blend. For a moister coating, add a little of the reserved cooking water. Serve immediately in warmed shallow bowls. At the table, season with salt and pepper to taste, passing the cheese.

# Tagliatelle with Beef Tenderloin, Bacon, and Italian Prunes

This rich, full-flavored pasta is great for entertaining. It goes together quickly with all kinds of interesting flavor notes. The Italian prunes add a touch of sweetness and depth; the juniper berries give an earthy, peppery, almost bay leaf–like scent that complements the smoky bacon seasoning. If there's time, make the sauce a day ahead to let the flavors develop.

By the way, I don't remove the juniper berries because I like their taste. If you wish, you can add them to the sauce in a mesh tea ball. That way, they're easy to take out after the sauce has cooked. Also, while any good smoky bacon can be used in this recipe, Nodine's makes a juniper bacon that seems to be made for this dish (see Sources, page 128, under The Grateful Palate).

SERVES 4

4 to 6 thick bacon slices (4 to 6 ounces uncooked), cut crosswise into $^1/_2$-inch pieces

2 pounds beef tenderloin, cut into $1^1/_2$-inch cubes

1 cup chopped onion

1 cup beef stock or broth

1 cup Pinot Noir

6 large prunes, preferably Italian plum, pitted and cut into chunks

8 to 10 juniper berries, crushed lightly (see Note)

$^1/_2$ teaspoon dried thyme

1 pound dried tagliatelle or other wide ribbon pasta

1 cup chopped tender, young arugula leaves

Coarse (kosher) salt and freshly ground pepper

IN A DUTCH OVEN, cook the bacon pieces over low to medium-low heat, turning as needed to brown but not crisp. Using a slotted spoon, transfer to a paper towel to drain. Pour off the bacon drippings, reserving 3 tablespoons in the pan.

IN THE SAME DUTCH OVEN, brown the beef cubes in batches over medium-high heat, 6 minutes per batch. Using a slotted spoon, transfer the beef to a plate. Lower the heat to medium, add the onion and sauté until soft, stirring frequently, about 7 minutes. Increase the heat to medium-high, add the beef stock, and deglaze the pan, using a wooden spoon to scrape up any browned bits stuck to the bottom of the pan. Bring the stock to a boil, then stir in the wine. Add the beef, bacon, prunes, juniper berries, and thyme. Cover, reduce the heat to low, stirring occasionally, until the beef is tender, 30 to 45 minutes. If making ahead, cool, cover, and refrigerate for up to 3 days, or freeze for up to 3 months. To serve, reheat the sauce over medium-low heat.

MEANWHILE, prepare the pasta according to package directions. Using plenty of boiling salted water, cook the pasta until al dente (tender but firm to the bite).

DRAIN WELL and divide the pasta among 4 heated soup plates. Divide the meat among the plates and spoon the sauce over each serving. Garnish with arugula and serve. At the table, season with salt and pepper to taste.

Note: Juniper berries are available in most supermarkets in the spice section. Spice Islands is one brand that carries them.

# Spaghetti alla Carbonara

Some say spaghetti alla carbonara was a poor-man's dish in ancient Rome. Others think it was tossed together by soldiers in World War II as a way to use up black-market bacon and eggs. I have an image of charcoal makers in central Italy traveling to the Abruzzi forests for wood, picking up some simple food along the way, and cooking it alfresco. Today, this dish is still considered one of the great bacon-and-egg combinations. You'll discover why, with this more traditional recipe or the garlic and white wine variation that follows.

### SERVES 4 AS A FIRST COURSE, 2 AS AN ENTRÉE

4 to 6 thick bacon slices (4 to 6 ounces uncooked), cut crosswise into 1/2-inch pieces

2   tablespoons olive oil

2   cloves garlic, smashed

10 to 12 ounces dried spaghetti

2   eggs at room temperature (see Note)

1/2   cup grated Parmigiano-Reggiano cheese, plus more for serving

1/4   cup minced fresh flat-leaf parsley

Coarse (kosher) salt and freshly ground pepper

IN A MEDIUM HEAVY SKILLET, cook the bacon pieces over low to medium-low heat, turning as needed to brown but not crisp. Using a slotted spoon, transfer to a paper towel to drain.

MEANWHILE, in a small saucepan, heat the olive oil and garlic over medium-low heat, and sauté until the garlic is golden brown, 5 to 7 minutes. Discard the garlic and set the oil aside to cool.

PREPARE THE PASTA according to package directions. Using plenty of boiling salted water, cook the pasta until al dente (tender but firm to the bite). (Serving hint: As the pasta water heats, place your serving bowl or platter over the pot to warm it.)

MEANWHILE, in a small bowl, whisk together the eggs and the garlic-infused olive oil until light lemony in color.

DRAIN THE PASTA well but do not rinse. Immediately transfer the pasta to the warmed serving bowl, add the egg mixture, and toss. (The heat from the pasta helps cook the eggs.) Add the bacon and the $1/2$ cup cheese and toss again. Divide the pasta among heated soup plates, garnish with parsley, and serve immediately. At the table, pass additional cheese and season with salt and pepper to taste.

Note: It is important to use the freshest eggs possible that have been kept refrigerated and are free of cracks. Because of the possibility that the eggs may be undercooked, people in high-risk groups, such as the elderly, the very young, the chronically ill, and pregnant women, should use pasteurized eggs. See Other Sources (page 129) for pasteurized shell eggs, which undergo the same heating process as milk does to destroy harmful bacteria.

# SPAGHETTI ALLA CARBONARA VERSION 2

FOR A BIT MORE BITE, and a lot more garlic flavor, follow the previous recipe, eliminating the olive oil. Reserve 2 tablespoons bacon drippings in the skillet used to cook the bacon. Add 2 cloves minced garlic and sauté over medium heat until golden brown. Pour in $1/3$ cup white wine and deglaze the pan, using a wooden spoon to scrape up any browned bits stuck to the bottom of the pan. Simmer until the wine is reduced by half. Set aside to cool. In a small bowl, whisk together the eggs and wine mixture and proceed as directed.

# Linguine and Bacon with Vodka Sauce

Here's a terrific grown-up pasta sauce to fix when friends come over for dinner. To round out the meal, all you'll need is a nice green salad, a crusty bread to mop up every last drop of sauce, and a robust bottle of Chianti. The tomato-based sauce is unusually rich and complex because of the way the vodka and cream complement one another. If you taste the sauce right after adding the vodka, you may find the flavor too strong. Be patient. The magic takes place when you stir in the cream.

## SERVES 6

8    thick pepper bacon slices (8 ounces uncooked), cut crosswise into 1-inch pieces

1    medium onion, chopped

1/4 to 1/2 teaspoon red pepper flakes

1/2  teaspoon dried fennel seeds

1    can (28 ounces) crushed Italian plum tomatoes, preferably San Marzano, with juices

1 1/2 tablespoons tomato paste

1    cup vodka

1    pound dried linguine

1    cup heavy (whipping) cream, warmed

Coarse (kosher) salt and freshly ground pepper

Fresh basil leaves, torn into strips, for garnishing

**IN A MEDIUM HEAVY SKILLET,** cook the bacon pieces over low to medium-low heat, turning as needed to achieve uniform crispness. Using a slotted spoon, transfer to a paper towel to drain. Pour off the bacon drippings, reserving 2 tablespoons in the skillet along with the coarse pepper that has come off the bacon pieces. Crumble one-third of the bacon for garnishing.

**IN THE SAME SKILLET,** add the onion, red pepper flakes, and fennel seeds to the reserved drippings. Cook over low to medium-low heat until the onion is very soft, 10 to 12 minutes. Stir in the tomatoes, tomato paste, vodka, and bacon pieces. Simmer, stirring frequently, for about 30 minutes.

**PREPARE THE PASTA** according to package directions. Using plenty of boiling salted water, cook the pasta until al dente (tender but firm to the bite). Drain well and divide the pasta among heated soup plates.

**MEANWHILE,** stir the cream into the sauce. Taste and adjust seasonings with cream and salt and pepper. Ladle the thick sauce down the center of each serving. Garnish with a line of basil on either side of the sauce. Sprinkle with the reserved bacon and serve.

## Variation:

## FOR LINGUINE, BACON, AND SAUSAGE WITH VODKA SAUCE,

follow the recipe above, adding 3 or 4 cooked Italian sausages, cut into 1-inch pieces, with the vodka. Then proceed as directed.

# Creamy Polenta with Bacon-Tomato-Corn Ragout

Into every bacon disciple's life a tried-and-true vegetarian will pass. This is not the time for preaching or conversion; it's more about living, loving, *and* eating together. Even if you're taken with bacon and your partner isn't, with this recipe you can dine in harmony. That's because the bacon is used as an optional seasoning and garnish. (Should your partner's palate awaken to bacon, try the variation on the next page.)

For a flavor that can't be beat, save this dish for summer. Use garden-fresh corn, vine-ripened heirloom tomatoes, and peppery basil.

## SERVES 2

2 to 4 thick bacon slices (2 to 4 ounces uncooked), cut crosswise into $1/2$-inch pieces (optional)
1 to 2 tablespoons olive oil
1   medium onion, sliced
Pinch of red pepper flakes
1   cup fresh corn kernels (about 2 ears) (see Note)
2   medium tomatoes, peeled, cored, and coarsely chopped (see Note)
$1/3$   cup chopped fresh basil
3   cups vegetable broth or water, or a combination
Pinch of crumbled dried thyme
1   teaspoon coarse (kosher) salt
$3/4$   cup quick-cooking polenta
$1/4$   cup fresh basil leaves, torn into strips
$1 1/2$ to 2 teaspoons fleur de sel or other large-grain finishing salt (optional)
Parmesan-Bacon Fricos for garnishing (optional; recipe follows)

**IN A MEDIUM HEAVY SKILLET,** cook the bacon pieces, over low to medium-low heat, turning as needed to achieve uniform crispness. Using a slotted spoon, transfer to a paper towel to drain.

**MEANWHILE,** in a large skillet, heat the olive oil over medium heat. Add the onion and red pepper flakes, reduce the heat to medium-low, and sauté until the onion is soft and amber, at least 20 minutes. Add the corn, increase the heat to medium, and cook for 5 minutes. Stir in the tomatoes and three-fourths of the bacon pieces, if desired, and continue to cook, stirring frequently, for 5 minutes. Stir in the basil.

**IN A MEDIUM HEAVY SAUCEPAN,** combine the broth, thyme, and salt. Bring to a boil and add the polenta in a slow stream, whisking constantly. Reduce the heat to low and simmer, whisking constantly, until the polenta thickens and pulls away from the sides of the pan, 4 to 6 minutes. Remove from heat and let sit, uncovered, for 1 minute. Divide the polenta between 2 bowls. Top with the ragout, basil, and a sprinkling of fleur de sel salt or the remaining bacon pieces. Serve with Parmesan-Bacon Fricos, if desired.

➡

**Note:** To remove corn kernels from the cob, cut off a small slice at the base so it stands flat. Hold the cob upright on a sturdy, clean surface. Using a sharp knife, cut downward, 3 or 4 rows at a time. Using the back of the knife, scrape the milk from the cob into a bowl. Add the corn to the bowl and use as directed.

**To peel a tomato**, cut an X-shaped slit on the bottom and drop it into a pot of boiling water for 5 to 10 seconds. (In this recipe, I use the broth or water in which I'll be cooking the polenta.) Using a slotted spoon, remove the tomato and set it on a clean towel to cool. (In other recipes, you may want to stop the cooking by plunging the tomato into ice water for 1 minute.) When the tomato is cool enough to handle, use a paring knife to remove the peel.

## Variation:

### FOR DON'T FORSAKEN THE BACON (AND CHEESE),

follow the recipe on page 59, eliminating the olive oil. Reserve 2 tablespoon bacon drippings in the skillet used to cook the bacon. Add the onion and red pepper flakes and proceed as directed. When preparing the polenta, substitute low-sodium chicken broth for the vegetable broth. After the polenta and broth have cooked for 4 minutes, stir in $1/2$ pound grated Fontina cheese until smooth. Spoon into bowls, top with ragout, basil, salt or bacon pieces and garnish or serve with Parmesan-Bacon Fricos. Pass additional grated Parmigiano-Reggiano cheese, if desired.

# Parmesan-Bacon Fricos

**These crisp cheese-and-bacon wafers are irresistible. Delicious as appetizers, they also make a festive garnish for thick polentas and stews. For easy entertaining, make them up to 3 days ahead and store in an airtight container.**

### MAKES 8

8   ounce wedge of Parmigiano-Reggiano cheese
2   crisply cooked thick bacon slices (2 ounces uncooked), cut into bits

**PREHEAT** the oven to 400°F. Line a baking sheet with parchment paper. Lightly brush with oil and dust with flour, shaking off the excess.

**USING THE MEDIUM HOLES ON A GRATER,** grate the cheese. In a small bowl, mix together the cheese and bacon until blended.

**SPRINKLE OR SPREAD** $1/2$ cup of the cheese mixture in a 6-inch circle. (You want to sprinkle enough cheese so it sticks together but doesn't destroy the lacy appearance.) Bake until the cheese turns golden, 8 to 10 minutes. Slide the parchment from the sheet to a wire rack to cool. Gently peel the cheese from the paper, a little at a time. Repeat process with remaining cheese mixture.

# Risotto with Spicy Pepper Bacon and Marsala

There's really no secret to great risotto, just a few self-evident truths: Use Italian Arborio rice; don't add too much liquid at one time (and not until the previous liquid has been absorbed); and enjoy the simple act of stirring. You'll be rewarded. This hearty risotto with its infusion of pepper bacon and Marsala makes a superb main-dish meal.

**SERVES 4 AS A FIRST COURSE, 2 AS AN ENTRÉE**

6   thick bacon slices (6 ounces uncooked), cut crosswise into 1-inch pieces
1   cup dry Marsala
3/4   cup minced onion
1   cup Arborio rice
4 to 4 1/2 cups hot chicken broth
3   tablespoons grated Parmigiano-Reggiano cheese
1   tablespoon unsalted butter
Coarse (kosher) salt and freshly ground pepper

**IN A MEDIUM HEAVY SKILLET,** cook the bacon pieces over low to medium-low heat, turning as needed to achieve uniform crispness. Using a slotted spoon, transfer to a paper towel to drain. Pour off all the bacon drippings, reserving 2 tablespoons in a bowl. Crumble the bacon and set aside.

**SET THE SKILLET** over medium-high to high heat, pour in 1/2 cup of the Marsala, and deglaze the pan, using a wooden spoon to scrape up any browned bits stuck to the bottom of the pan. Reduce the heat to medium and simmer until the liquid is reduced by half. Set aside.

**IN A 2- TO 2 1/2-QUART HEAVY-BOTTOMED SAUCEPAN,** heat the reserved drippings over medium heat, add the onion, and sauté until translucent, 3 to 4 minutes. Add the rice and increase the heat to medium-high. Stir vigorously until the kernels are translucent and you can see "the eye" at the tip of the kernel. (Do not let the rice brown.)

**ADD THE REMAINING 1/2 CUP MARSALA** to the rice mixture, stirring the rice away from the bottom and sides until the liquid is evaporated. Add the hot broth, 1/2 cup at a time, stirring constantly, until the liquid is absorbed and the rice does not stick or burn. After you've used half to three-fourths of the broth, stir in the reduced Marsala and half the crumbled bacon. Add the remaining broth, 1/4 cup at a time, stirring constantly.

**TASTE THE RICE** after 20 minutes. It should be tender but firm to the bite, and the mixture slightly moist and porridgelike. If it's not tender enough, continue to cook and taste again in 3 to 5 minutes. Remove from heat and stir in the cheese and butter. Season with salt and pepper to taste. Mound the risotto into warmed shallow bowls, top with the remaining crumbled bacon, and serve steaming hot.

# THE ULTIMATE SIDEKICK

Sure, I'll eat my vegetables . . . with bacon

# Sweet Onions Roasted with Bacon, Balsamic Vinegar, and Herbes de Provence

**Wedges of sweet onions and bacon pieces are drizzled with a balsamic–maple syrup vinaigrette and herbes de Provence for a deep, heady flavor. This is a great dish to serve alongside a roasted pork tenderloin.**

### SERVES 4

6 to 8 thick smoked bacon slices (6 to 8 ounces uncooked), cut crosswise into 2-inch pieces

2    large sweet onions, such as Walla Walla, Vidalia, or Maui, peeled and each cut into 6 or 8 wedges with root-end intact

2¹⁄₂ tablespoons balsamic vinegar

2¹⁄₂ tablespoons water, plus more as needed

2    teaspoons pure maple syrup

2    tablespoons olive oil

1    teaspoon herbes de Provence (see Note)

Coarse (kosher) salt and freshly ground pepper

**PREHEAT** the oven to 400°F.

**IN A MEDIUM HEAVY SKILLET,** cook the bacon pieces over low to medium-low heat, turning as needed until they just begin to brown.

**MEANWHILE,** put the onion wedges in a 9-by-13-inch baking pan. Using a slotted spoon, transfer the bacon pieces to the pan, tucking them between the onion wedges.

**IN A SMALL BOWL,** whisk together the vinegar, 2¹⁄₂ tablespoons water, maple syrup, oil, and herbes de Provence. Pour the mixture over the onions and bacon. Season with salt and pepper to taste. Roast the onions, basting frequently and adding 1 tablespoon water at a time if the marinade begins to evaporate. Cook until tender and covered with a syrupy glaze, about 45 minutes. Serve the onion wedges hot or at room temperature, making sure to include bacon pieces and pan drippings with each serving.

**Note:** Herbes de Provence, a favorite in southern France, can be found already blended in the spice section of most supermarkets. If unavailable, substitute a pinch of dried basil, marjoram, rosemary, sage, and/or lavender.

# Green Beans with Crispy Bacon and Lemon Zest

**A quick sauté, some scrumptious pepper bacon, and ribbons of lemon zest make this a simple and flavorful dish for showing off the green beans of early summer. I like to use Blue Lake or French haricots verts; they're tender and sweet and require very little cooking. With this combination, you may even get your kids to eat their vegetables.**

## SERVES 4

4     thick pepper bacon slices (4 ounces uncooked), cut diagonally into 1/2-inch pieces

1     pound young green beans, trimmed

1 to 2 tablespoons water

Zest of 1 large lemon (see Note)

2     tablespoons fresh lemon juice

Lemon pepper (optional)

Coarse (kosher) salt and freshly ground black pepper (optional)

**IN A MEDIUM HEAVY SKILLET,** cook the bacon pieces over low to medium-low heat, turning as needed to achieve uniform crispness. Using a slotted spoon, transfer to a paper towel to drain. Pour off the bacon drippings, reserving 1 tablespoon in the skillet.

**IN THE SAME SKILLET,** increase the heat to medium-high, add the green beans, and toss in the drippings until coated. Sauté, stirring frequently, adding 1 tablespoon water at a time, to keep the beans moist and prevent them from browning. Cook until just tender-crisp, 4 to 5 minutes. Sprinkle the beans with the bacon, the lemon zest, and lemon juice. Toss and sauté for 30 seconds. Season with lemon pepper or salt and black pepper to taste, if desired, and serve.

 **Note:** Instead of using a grater, use a 4- or 5-hole zester to create 1/2- to 1-inch-long ribbons.

67

# One-Potato, Two-Potato, Baked Potato

Potatoes are the world's best vegetable (yes, I know they're tubers), and one potato, twice baked, with loads of bacon, is the best excuse I know for eating your vegetables. If you really want a Yankee feast, add a poached egg on top and enjoy the whole thing with a bottle of Samuel Adams Pale Ale or Golden Pilsner. That's my idea of heaven.

**SERVES 4**

4    medium Idaho or baking potatoes, scrubbed
3    thick bacon slices (3 ounces uncooked),
     cut crosswise into $1/2$-inch pieces
4    tablespoons finely minced shallots
1    cup (4 ounces) grated sharp white Cheddar
     cheese, preferably White Diamond
1    cup sour cream
2    teaspoons finely chopped chives
Coarse (kosher) salt and freshly ground pepper
Sweet paprika for sprinkling

**PREHEAT** the oven to 400°F.

**WITH A FORK OR SKEWER,** prick the potatoes several times. Place the potatoes on an oven rack, and bake until they give and are soft when gently squeezed with a towel, about 1 hour.

**MEANWHILE,** in a medium heavy skillet, cook the bacon pieces over low to medium-low heat, turning as needed to achieve uniform crispness. Using a slotted spoon, transfer to a paper towel to drain. Pour off the bacon drippings, reserving 2 tablespoons in the skillet. Coarsely chop the bacon and set aside.

**IN THE SAME SKILLET,** add the shallots and sauté over medium-low heat until translucent and tender, 3 to 4 minutes. Using a slotted spoon, transfer to a medium bowl.

**WHEN THE POTATOES** are cool enough to handle, using a sharp paring knife, cut an oval lid one-third of the way from each end, discarding the lid. Using a soup spoon, gently scoop out the flesh into the bowl with the shallots, leaving a $1/8$- to $1/4$-inch layer of the potato in the shell. Be careful not to tear through the skin. Mix together the potato and shallots. Put the potato mixture through a ricer or food mill into a clean bowl.

**ADD THE CHEESE,** sour cream, chives, and salt and pepper to taste. Holding a potato-skin shell with one hand, use a spoon or small rubber spatula to fill the shell with the potato mixture, mounding it 1 inch above the rim. (If there is extra filling, place it in a greased small ramekin, cover, and refrigerate it for baking another time.) Using the end of a finger, create a center trough or crevice through the length of the stuffing, smoothing the outer edges and sides, then sprinkle with paprika.Place the potatoes on a rimmed baking sheet. Bake until heated through, about 30 minutes. Remove and generously fill the troughs with the bacon. Serve immediately.

# Corn and Clam Chowder with Bacon

This nourishing chowder is a wonderful soup, with or without the cream. There's a hint of the unfamiliar that makes you want to take another spoonful, and another. Crushing the fennel together with the thyme creates the intriguing flavor.

**SERVES 4**

1/4  teaspoon fennel seeds

1/2  teaspoon dried thyme

6    thick smoked bacon slices (6 ounces uncooked),
     cut crosswise into 1-inch pieces

1    medium onion, cut into 1/4-inch dice

2    tablespoons all-purpose flour

3 1/2 cups chicken broth

2    cups fresh or frozen corn kernels

3/4  pound medium thin-skinned white potatoes,
     cut into 1/4-inch dice

1    can (6 ounces) chopped clam meat,
     drained (about 1/2 cup)

1    cup heavy (whipping) cream, heated

Coarse (kosher) salt and freshly ground pepper

1/4  cup chopped fresh flat-leaf parsley for garnishing

**USING A MORTAR AND PESTLE,** mini-prep processor, or coffee grinder, crush or grind the fennel seeds and thyme together. (If you use a coffee grinder, be sure to wipe it out afterward.)

**IN A 2- TO 2 1/2-QUART HEAVY SAUCEPAN** or Dutch oven, cook the bacon pieces over low to medium-low heat, turning as needed to achieve uniform crispness. Using a slotted spoon, transfer to a paper towel to drain. Pour off the bacon drippings, reserving 2 tablespoons in the saucepan. Chop the bacon into small pieces and set aside.

**IN THE SAME SAUCEPAN,** add the onion and sauté over medium heat, stirring frequently, until soft, about 5 minutes. Sprinkle on the flour and the fennel mixture and cook for 1 minute, stirring constantly. Stir in the broth, corn, and potatoes. Bring to a boil, reduce the heat to a simmer, and cook until the potatoes are tender, 10 to 15 minutes. Stir in the clams and cream and heat through. Season with salt and pepper to taste. Ladle into warmed shallow soup plates or bowls. Garnish with bacon and parsley.

69

# Marvelous Mashed Potatoes with Bacon

For those who think there's nothing better than mashed potatoes *with* dinner, do I have news for you! The best thing *for* dinner is a plateful of these marvelous mashed potatoes with bacon. Oh, sure, if you want to add a beef brochette, a lamb kabob, or a piece of grilled chicken or salmon, go ahead, but you don't need to. Just make a small green salad and pour yourself a glass of wine. The combination of creamy mashed potatoes and nutty Fontina cheese with the bacon and spinach is so satisfying.

**SERVES 4 AS A SIDE DISH, 2 AS AN ENTRÉE**

4 to 6 thick slices smoked bacon (4 to 6 ounces uncooked), cut crosswise into ¹/₂-inch pieces

2 pounds Idaho or baking potatoes, peeled and cut into ¹/₃-inch-thick slices

6 ounces baby spinach

2 tablespoons milk, warmed

3 tablespoons unsalted butter

1 cup (3¹/₂ to 4 ounces) grated Fontina cheese

Coarse (kosher) salt and freshly ground pepper

**IN A MEDIUM HEAVY SKILLET,** cook the bacon pieces over low to medium-low heat, turning as needed to achieve uniform crispness. Using a slotted spoon, transfer to a paper towel to drain.

**IN A LARGE SAUCEPAN,** cover the potatoes with cold, salted water. Bring to a boil over medium-high heat. Reduce the heat to a simmer and cook until the potatoes are tender, 20 to 30 minutes. Drain the potatoes for 1 to 2 minutes, letting the steam rise and the potatoes dry out.

**MEANWHILE,** remove the stems from the spinach, rinse, and lightly shake. Put the spinach in a steamer over boiling water, or put it in a heavy pan, cover, and cook over medium heat, shaking the pan several times, until wilted, 2 to 3 minutes. Drain well. Cool slightly and squeeze out as much moisture as possible. Set aside.

**PUT THE POTATOES** through a ricer or food mill into a large bowl or the saucepan. Add the milk and butter and stir until smooth. Add the cheese, spinach, and bacon and stir until the cheese melts. Season with salt and pepper to taste and serve immediately.

# The Best Baked Beans

At my house, baked beans were served in the summer when Dad fired up the barbecue. Mom would open a can of B&M baked beans and doctor them with blackstrap molasses, Heinz ketchup, and Coleman's dry mustard. The only drawback was that big cube of pork fat, which always seemed to end up on my plate.

One of the great things about being a grown-up is the chance to fool around in your kitchen and recapture that childhood dish, adding your own culinary signature. The baked beans in this recipe have all the sweet syrupy goodness of the archetypal baked beans plus the added zing of fresh ginger. The best part? To forgo the cube of pork fat and use plenty of great-tasting bacon.

**SERVES 4**

2   cups dried navy beans
3 or 4 fresh thyme sprigs
1   bay leaf, broken
1-by-1-inch chunk of fresh ginger, peeled
    and cut into 4 pieces
8   thick smoked bacon slices (8 ounces uncooked),
    cut crosswise into 1-inch pieces
2   medium onions, chopped (about 2$^1/_2$ cups)
$^1/_3$   cup dark molasses
4   tablespoons bourbon

3   tablespoons Dijon mustard
$^1/_3$   cup tomato paste
2   teaspoons cider vinegar
2   tablespoons Worcestershire sauce
2 to 4 cups hot apple cider (not juice)
Coarse (kosher) salt and freshly ground pepper

**PUT THE BEANS** in a Dutch oven with enough cold water to cover. Bring to a boil over medium heat. Then drain and rinse the beans, and return them to the Dutch oven with enough cold water to cover. Bring to a boil again. Reduce the heat to a simmer and cook for 30 minutes, skimming off any foam. Drain the beans and set aside.

**PREHEAT** the oven to 325°F. Put the thyme, bay leaf, and ginger into a large mesh tea ball.

**IN THE DUTCH OVEN,** cook the bacon pieces over low to medium-low heat, turning as needed until the bacon just begins to brown. Using a slotted spoon, transfer to a paper towel to drain. Pour off the bacon drippings, reserving $^1/_4$ cup in the Dutch oven.

**IN THE DUTCH OVEN,** add the onions and cook over medium heat until translucent, 3 to 4 minutes. Add the beans, bacon, molasses, bourbon, mustard, tomato paste, vinegar, Worcestershire sauce, and 2 cups of the cider, and stir to blend. Add the tea ball, making sure to submerge it. Bake, covered, for 2$^1/_2$ hours, adding more cider as needed to keep the mixture from drying out. Uncover and bake for an additional 1$^1/_2$ hours, continuing to add more cider as needed. Remove the tea ball and season the beans with salt and pepper to taste.

# Bacon-Ricotta Gratin with Tomatoes and Zucchini

In this warm and savory gratin, thin zucchini rounds, Italian plum tomatoes, and sautéed onions are snuggled under a blanket of savory cheese custard. The thick, smoky bacon pieces provide the ideal counterpoint. Enjoy this dish as a first course, a light entrée, or an accompaniment to a roasted chicken or pork tenderloin.

*Psst!* You may want to slip this recipe into the files of certain friends and relatives—the ones who are staggering under loads of zucchini from their gardens. Who knows, there's a chance you'll be served this instead of zucchini bread.

**SERVES 4**

6     thick unsmoked bacon slices (6 ounces uncooked), cut crosswise into 1/2-inch pieces

1     medium onion, chopped

1     large clove garlic, finely minced

1     can (14.5 ounces) whole peeled Italian plum tomatoes, drained

1     tablespoon finely chopped fresh basil or 2 teaspoons dried basil

Pinch of nutmeg

Coarse (kosher) salt and freshly ground pepper

1     tablespoon unsalted butter

3     cups thinly sliced zucchini (about 3/4 pound)

2     eggs

1     cup ricotta cheese, drained through a sieve if watery

1     cup half-and-half

1     cup grated Parmigiano-Reggiano or Pecorino Romano cheese

**PREHEAT** the oven to 450°F.

**IN A MEDIUM HEAVY SKILLET,** cook the bacon pieces over low to medium-low heat, turning as needed to achieve uniform crispness. Using a slotted spoon, transfer to a paper towel to drain. Pour off the bacon drippings, reserving 2 tablespoons in the skillet.

**IN THE SAME SKILLET,** add the onion and sauté over medium heat until soft, about 8 minutes. Add the garlic and sauté for 2 minutes. Add the tomatoes, basil, nutmeg, and salt and pepper to taste. Simmer, stirring occasionally, until most of the liquid evaporates, about 5 minutes.

**IN A LARGE SAUTÉ PAN,** melt the butter over medium heat. When it begins to foam, add the zucchini and sauté until tender-crisp, about 6 minutes. Using a slotted spoon, transfer the zucchini to a paper towel to drain.

**IN A LARGE BOWL,** whisk the eggs for 10 seconds. Whisk in the ricotta, half-and-half, and three-fourths of the Parmigiano-Reggiano cheese.

**TO ASSEMBLE,** layer half of the zucchini slices on the bottom of a 9-by-1$^{1}/_{2}$-inch quiche dish. Spread the tomato mixture over the zucchini. Sprinkle the bacon over the tomatoes and layer the remaining zucchini on top. Pour the egg mixture over all the layers, then sprinkle on the remaining cheese.

**BAKE** for 12 minutes. Reduce the temperature to 375°F, and continue to bake until the gratin is puffed and beginning to brown, about 25 minutes. Transfer to a wire rack to cool for 10 minutes. To serve, cut into wedges.

# Autumn Soup with Cinnamon-Pepper Croutons

**This soup is a great pleasure on a cold night. When there's company, I always take the extra step of passing the soup through a fine sieve. The texture is velvety and quite elegant. When it's family, we like to briefly purée the soup in the food processor so it's barely chunky.**

## SERVES 4

4   thick smoked bacon slices (4 ounces uncooked), cut crosswise into 1-inch pieces, or 4 ounces slab bacon, cut into $^{1}/_{2}$-inch cubes
1   large onion, chopped
$^{1}/_{2}$   cup dry Marsala
4   cups low-sodium chicken broth
2   cloves garlic
2   small garnet yams (about 1$^{1}/_{2}$ pounds total), cut into 1-inch pieces
6   fresh thyme sprigs
2   fresh sage sprigs
1   fresh rosemary sprig
1   teaspoon Worcestershire sauce
Dash of Tabasco sauce
Coarse (kosher) salt and freshly ground pepper
Cinnamon-Pepper Croutons (recipe follows)

IN A MEDIUM HEAVY SKILLET, cook the bacon pieces over low to medium-low heat, turning as needed to brown but not crisp. Using a slotted spoon, transfer to a paper towel to drain. Pour off the bacon drippings, reserving 2 tablespoons in the skillet. Chop the bacon into small pieces, reserving $^1/_4$ cup for garnishing.

IN THE SAME SKILLET, add the onion and sauté over medium heat until browned and tender, 5 to 7 minutes. Stir in the Marsala and simmer until the liquid is reduced by half, about 3 minutes.

IN A MEDIUM SAUCEPAN, combine the onion and any drippings from the skillet with the broth, garlic, and yams. Put the thyme, sage, and rosemary in a 2-inch mesh tea ball, or tie the sprigs with cotton string, and add to the pan. Bring the mixture to a boil, then reduce the heat to a simmer. Cook until the yams are soft, 15 to 20 minutes. Cool slightly.

IN A FOOD PROCESSOR, working in batches, purée the soup. Or pass it through a food mill. For a velvety texture, pass the soup through a fine sieve. It takes longer but is worth the time and trouble. Return the soup to the saucepan, stir in the Worcestershire, Tabasco, and salt and pepper to taste. Garnish each serving with bacon and Cinnamon-Pepper Croutons.

# CINNAMON-PEPPER CROUTONS

### MAKES ABOUT 1$^1/_3$ CUPS

| | |
|---|---|
| 2 | cups fresh bread cubes ($^1/_4$-inch cubes) |
| 4 | teaspoons olive oil |
| $^1/_4$ | teaspoon freshly ground pepper |
| $^3/_4$ | teaspoon ground cinnamon |
| 1 | teaspoon sugar |

PREHEAT the oven to 375°F or use a toaster oven.

IN A MEDIUM BOWL, drizzle the bread cubes with the olive oil and toss well with your hands. In a cup, mix together the pepper, cinnamon, and sugar. Sprinkle the pepper mixture over the bread cubes and toss. Toast, tossing with a spatula several times, until crisp, about 10 minutes. The croutons can be made up to 1 week in advance and stored in an airtight container.

# Jane's Bacon and Lentil Soup

Oregon artist Jane Zwinger is a master with pen, paper, and brush. She also has the expert's touch with a knife, Dutch oven, and spoon, creating heavenly soups and stews. She'll concoct a new recipe on the weekend so that when she's in her studio or on the site of her next mural, her Thermos will be brimming with a satisfying masterpiece.

**SERVES 4**

3/4    cup small red lentils
1      bay leaf
4      cups water
10 to 12 thick smoked bacon slices (10 to 12 ounces
       uncooked), cut crosswise into 1-inch pieces
1      small onion, cut into 1/4-inch dice
1      small carrot, peeled and cut into 1/8-inch slices
2      medium celery stalks, cut into 1/8-inch slices
1      clove garlic, minced
1      can (14.5 ounces) diced tomatoes
1/2    teaspoon dried oregano
1/2    teaspoon cumin
2      tablespoons coarsely chopped fresh mint
Coarse (kosher) salt and freshly ground pepper
1      green onion, both white and green parts,
       thinly sliced

**IN A MEDIUM SAUCEPAN,** stir together the lentils, bay leaf, and water. Bring to a boil, reduce the heat to a simmer, and cook until the lentils are soft, about 20 minutes.

**MEANWHILE,** in a medium heavy skillet, cook the bacon pieces over low to medium-low heat, turning as needed to brown but not crisp. Using a slotted spoon, transfer to a paper towel to drain. Pour off the bacon drippings, reserving 1 tablespoon in the skillet. Chop the bacon into small pieces and set aside.

**IN THE SAME SKILLET,** add the onion and sauté over medium heat until tender and starting to brown, 5 to 7 minutes. Add the carrot, celery, and garlic and sauté until tender, about 5 minutes. Add the onion mixture and the tomatoes to the lentils and stir until blended. Stir in the chopped bacon (reserving 1/4 cup for garnishing), the oregano, cumin, and mint. Remove the bay leaf, and season with salt and pepper to taste. Simmer for 10 minutes. Garnish each serving with the sliced green onion and reserved bacon.

# CLASSIC AND FORBIDDEN PLEASURES

Must-have dishes and lusty antidotes
to life in the no-fun lane

# Gorgonzola Cheeseburgers with Bacon

C'mon, we all know bacon cheeseburgers are the reason hamburgers were invented in the first place. A cruise through any fast-food line confirms it. But honestly, who wants limp bacon slices, thin burgers stamped from a mold, and cheese whose origin is questionable? Give me something real with heft, bite, and flavor. Something juicy, creamy, and crunchy. Something to sink my teeth into.

Ahh, you found the Gorgonzola! Great, isn't it?

**SERVES 2**

4     thick bacon slices (4 ounces uncooked)
1     medium red or yellow onion, peeled and cut into rings
12    ounces ground sirloin or chuck
1 1/2 teaspoons Worcestershire sauce
Coarse (kosher) salt and freshly ground pepper
1     wedge (3 ounces) Gorgonzola cheese, sliced
4     sourdough bread slices, toasted
Ripe tomato slices for serving
Tender, young arugula leaves for serving

**PREHEAT** the oven to 200°F.

**IN A MEDIUM HEAVY SKILLET,** place the bacon slices in a single layer and cook over low to medium-low heat, turning as needed to achieve uniform crispness. Transfer to a paper towel to drain. Pour off the bacon drippings, reserving 1 to 2 tablespoons in the skillet.

**IN THE SAME SKILLET,** add the onion and sauté over medium heat, stirring frequently, until soft, 12 to 20 minutes. The longer you can cook the onion without overbrowning, the sweeter and tastier it will be. Transfer to an ovenproof plate and place in the oven to keep warm.

**MEANWHILE,** put the meat in a medium bowl, drizzle with the Worcestershire sauce, and gently form into 2 oval or round patties, about 1/2 inch thick. Season both sides with salt and pepper to taste. In the same skillet or on a griddle, cook the patties over medium-high heat until well browned on one side, about 2 minutes. Turn the burgers and top each with sliced cheese. Cover and cook until the cheese melts and the burgers are medium-rare to medium (140°F to 155°F), 2 to 3 minutes. (Note: USDA recommends 160°F or medium-well, to kill any potential bacteria.)

**TO SERVE,** place each burger, cheese-side up, on 1 bread slice. Cover each burger with half of the bacon slices, onions, tomatoes, and arugula. Set remaining bread slices on top, gently press, and serve.

# BLT with Green Herb Mayonnaise

The three most important letters in a bacon-lover's alphabet add up to one classic sandwich. But to be truly great, it must be made with the best ingredients you can find—sun-ripened heirloom tomatoes, sweet leafy green lettuce, your favorite bread, and a really splendid bacon. (This book can help you there. See Sources, page 128.)

One other thing. When it comes to the sandwich spread, some people swear by Best Foods mayonnaise; others only touch Miracle Whip. Since you've gone to the trouble of using the finest ingredients, you might want to make your own spread. I've included a tasty homemade herb mayonnaise that is good plain or seasoned. But there's nothing wrong with unscrewing that blue lid, and spreading it on thick.

**SERVES 1**

2    good-quality white sandwich bread slices, toasted

2    tablespoons mayonnaise, preferably Green Herb Mayonnaise (see page 84)

1/2  cup torn butter lettuce or tender, young arugula leaves

3    crisply cooked slices of your favorite bacon

1    medium vine-ripened tomato, cut into 1/4-inch slices

Coarse (kosher) salt and freshly ground pepper

**ON EACH BREAD SLICE,** spread equal amounts of the mayonnaise. Arrange half of the lettuce on 1 bread slice and top with the bacon. Arrange the remaining lettuce on the other bread slice and top with the tomato slices. Season the tomato with salt and pepper to taste. Press the bread slices gently together and cut in half diagonally. Transfer to a plate and serve. If you wish to serve it open-faced, assemble the sandwich on the plate.

# GREEN HERB MAYONNAISE

**Fresh herbs give this rich, creamy mayonnaise its bright, lively taste. If you prefer a plain mayonnaise, simply eliminate the herbs.**

**MAKES ABOUT 1¹/₂ CUPS**

| | |
|---|---|
| 1 | whole egg at room temperature (see Note) |
| 1 | egg yolk at room temperature |
| 2 | tablespoons fresh lemon juice |
| ¹/₂ | teaspoon coarse (kosher) salt |
| ²/₃ | cup vegetable or canola oil |
| ¹/₃ | cup mild-flavored olive oil |
| 1 | teaspoon dry mustard |
| ¹/₂ | teaspoon grated lemon zest |
| ¹/₄ | teaspoon fresh thyme leaves |
| ¹/₄ | teaspoon fresh marjoram leaves |
| 3 | tablespoons torn fresh basil |

**IN A BLENDER,** mix together the egg, egg yolk, lemon juice, and salt for 20 seconds. In a 1-cup liquid measuring cup, combine the vegetable and olive oils. Set the blender on mix or frappé and slowly add ¹/₄ cup oil, a drop at a time. As the mixture begins to thicken, drizzle in the remaining oil in a fine stream. As it thickens, it will become glossy. Blend in the mustard, lemon zest, thyme, marjoram, and basil until the mixture becomes light green. Taste and adjust seasonings with salt or lemon juice. Cover and refrigerate for 3 to 5 days.

**Note:** To bring a chilled egg to room temperature, immerse the whole egg in a small bowl of very warm water for 10 minutes.

**Safety Tip:** Since this mayonnaise contains raw egg, it is important to use the freshest eggs possible that are free of cracks and have been kept refrigerated. Since raw egg carries the risk of bacterial growth that can cause salmonella poisoning, it should not be served to people in high-risk groups, such as the elderly, the very young, the chronically ill, and pregnant women. See Other Sources (page 129) for pasteurized shell eggs, which undergo the same heating process as milk does to destroy harmful bacteria.

84

# Kentucky Hot Brown

Any Southerner worth his weight in bacon will tell you this sandwich is the definition of comfort food. It's soothing, filling, and not too taxing on the taste buds. Many swear it's best made with a soft and squishy schoolyard favorite—Wonder (a.k.a. balloon) Bread. I opt for a dense, rustic artisan-style bread. Whichever you choose, go for a hickory- or applewood-smoked bacon with plenty of flavor so it can finesse the billowy cheese sauce.

**SERVES 4**

3 tablespoons unsalted butter
2 tablespoons minced shallots
3 tablespoons all-purpose flour
2 cups milk
1/2 to 1 cup (2 to 4 ounces) grated Cheddar cheese
1/2 teaspoon Worcestershire sauce
Coarse (kosher) salt and white pepper
Pinch of nutmeg
8 good-quality white bread slices, toasted
1 pound thinly sliced turkey or chicken breast
Paprika for dusting
1 cup crumbled crisply cooked bacon
   (1 pound uncooked)
2 small ripe tomatoes, chopped (optional)
1 1/2 tablespoons chopped fresh flat-leaf parsley
   (optional)

**IN A SMALL SAUCEPAN,** melt the butter over medium-low heat. Add the shallots and sauté until soft, about 5 minutes. Whisk in the flour and cook, whisking constantly, until the mixture begins to darken, about 3 minutes. Slowly whisk in the milk in a steady stream until blended and smooth. Reduce the heat to low and continue to cook, whisking until thickened, about 3 minutes. Sprinkle in the grated cheese, and whisk until blended and smooth. Remove from heat, season with the Worcestershire, salt, pepper, and nutmeg to taste, and set aside briefly. (To keep the sauce warm for up to 1 hour, transfer it to the top pan of a double boiler over simmering water. Be sure to stir occasionally.)

**PREHEAT** the broiler.

**TRIM OFF** the bread crusts. Cut 4 slices in half diagonally. Leave the remaining 4 slices as squares. To assemble, place 1 toast square in the middle of each of 4 ovenproof serving plates. Arrange 2 toast diagonals on opposite sides of each square with points turned outward. Top each toast square with sliced turkey. Cover with cheese sauce.

**BROIL** the sandwiches until the sauce begins to bubble and brown, 1/2 to 1 minute. Watch carefully; browning time will vary depending on the thickness of the sandwich. Remove with oven mitts. Dust the sandwiches with paprika and garnish with bacon and tomatoes and parsley, if desired. Serve immediately.

# Club Sandwich with Lemon-Caper and Chipotle-Lime Mayonnaises

The club sandwich remains one of America's all-time culinary classics that always tastes better with bacon. For this version, I've added a new twist: two different mayonnaise spreads to spark new interest.

**SERVES 1**

3  good-quality white bread slices, lightly toasted
1  tablespoon Lemon-Caper Mayonnaise (recipe follows)
3  iceberg or butter lettuce leaves, each about 4 inches square
2  ounces thinly sliced turkey or chicken breast
1 1/2  teaspoons Chipotle-Lime Mayonnaise (recipe follows) or Green Herb Mayonnaise (see page 84)
2  thick vine-ripened tomato slices, peeled and seeded (optional)
3  crisply cooked thick smoked bacon slices (3 ounces uncooked)
Coarse (kosher) salt and freshly ground pepper

**ON 2 OF THE BREAD SLICES,** spread equal amounts of the Lemon-Caper Mayonnaise. Top 1 slice with 1 lettuce leaf and the turkey. Spread the Chipotle-Lime Mayonnaise on the remaining bread slice and place it on top of the turkey, mayonnaise-side up. Top with 1 lettuce leaf, tomato (if desired), bacon, and the remaining lettuce leaf. Season with salt and pepper to taste. Top with the remaining bread slice, Lemon-Caper Mayonnaise–side down. Gently press the bread slices together and cut into 4 triangles. Transfer to a plate, pierce each triangle with a toothpick, and serve.

## LEMON-CAPER MAYONNAISE

**MAKES ABOUT 1 1/2 CUPS**

1  whole egg at room temperature (see Note)
1  egg yolk at room temperature
2  tablespoons plus 1 teaspoon fresh lemon juice
1/2  teaspoon coarse (kosher) salt
2/3  cup vegetable or canola oil
1/3  cup mild-flavored olive oil
1  tablespoon plus 1 teaspoon capers, rinsed and drained
1/2  teaspoon pressed garlic
1/2  teaspoon grated lemon zest
White pepper (optional)

IN A BLENDER, mix together the egg, egg yolk, lemon juice, and salt for 20 seconds. In a 1-cup liquid measuring cup, combine the vegetable and olive oils. Set the blender on mix or frappé and slowly add ¼ cup oil, a drop at a time. As the mixture begins to thicken, drizzle in the remaining oil in a fine stream. As it thickens, it will become glossy. Blend in the capers, garlic, and lemon zest. Taste and adjust seasonings, adding white pepper, if desired. Cover and refrigerate for 3 to 5 days.

Note: Since this mayonnaise contains raw egg, be sure to read the Safety Tip on page 84.

To bring a chilled egg to room temperature, immerse the whole egg in a small bowl of very warm water for 10 minutes.

# CHIPOTLE-LIME MAYONNAISE

**Whether you like your seasoning fiery hot or simply spicy, it's a good idea to gradually add the second chile and the adobo sauce. That way, you can judge exactly what your taste buds can tolerate. Who knows, you may want to use this mayonnaise on every layer of the sandwich.**

**MAKES ABOUT 1½ CUPS**

1    whole egg at room temperature (see Note)
1    egg yolk at room temperature
2    tablespoons plus 1 teaspoon fresh lime juice

½    teaspoon coarse (kosher) salt
⅔    cup vegetable or canola oil
⅓    cup mild-flavored olive oil
¼    teaspoon dry mustard
Zest of 1 large lime, grated or minced
1 to 2 chipotle chiles in adobo sauce, seeded and
    chopped (see Note)
2 to 3 teaspoons adobo sauce (optional)

IN A BLENDER, mix together the egg, egg yolk, lime juice, and salt for 20 seconds. In a 1-cup liquid measuring cup, combine the vegetable and olive oils. Set the blender on mix or frappé and slowly add ¼ cup oil, a drop at a time. As the mixture begins to thicken, drizzle in the remaining oil in a fine stream. As it thickens, it will become glossy.

USING A RUBBER SPATULA, scrape the mayonnaise into a medium bowl. Whisk in the dry mustard and lime zest. Fold in 1 chopped chipotle. Taste and adjust seasonings, adding the additional chipotle and adobo sauce, if desired. Cover and refrigerate for 3 to 5 days.

Note: Since this mayonnaise contains raw egg, be sure to read the Safety Tip on page 84.

To bring a chilled egg to room temperature, immerse the whole egg in a small bowl of very warm water for 10 minutes.

Chipotle chiles in adobo sauce are available in 7-ounce cans in most supermarkets and Mexican grocery stores. For this recipe, remove 2 chiles from the thick sauce, rinse, slice open, and seed. If you're sensitive to chiles, wear gloves when handling them; the oils can cause a burning sensation on your skin.

# Peanut Butter and You-Guessed-It Sandwich

Try it—Elvis did—and, while you're at it, fix the other peanut butter and bacon variations I've listed below. You'll see, one of these combos will end up as a brown-bag favorite.

**SERVES 1**

2   white, whole-wheat, or raisin bread slices or bagel, fresh or lightly toasted

2 to 4 tablespoons creamy or chunky peanut butter

2   crisply cooked thin or thick bacon slices (1 to 2 ounces uncooked)

1   apple, such as Fuji or Jonagold, cored and thinly sliced

4 to 6 tender, young arugula leaves (optional)

**ON EACH BREAD SLICE,** spread equal amounts of the peanut butter. Layer the bacon slices on 1 bread slice. Layer the apple slices on the other bread slice and top with the arugula, if desired. Gently press the bread slices together.

## SANDWICH VARIATIONS

All you need is an achin' for bacon and 2 slices of fresh or lightly toasted bread or a bagel. Then, stick out your finger, close your eyes, point to the list below, and have some fun. Any one of these fillings will have you singing "Love Me Tender."

Peanut butter, orange marmalade, and crisply cooked bacon slices

Peanut butter, grape jelly, iceberg lettuce, and crisply cooked bacon slices

Peanut butter, honey, alfalfa sprouts, and crisply cooked bacon slices

Peanut butter, sliced sweet midget pickles, and crisply cooked bacon slices

Peanut butter mixed with 1 tablespoon minced sweet pickles and 1 teaspoon ketchup and crisply cooked bacon slices

Peanut butter, mayonnaise, and crisply cooked bacon slices

Peanut butter, tomato slices, and crisply cooked bacon slices

Peanut butter, mayonnaise, tomato slices, lettuce, and crisply cooked bacon slices

Peanut butter, mayonnaise or Miracle Whip, chopped red onion, sugar, and crisply cooked bacon slices

Peanut butter, pineapple ring, slice of American cheese, and crisply cooked bacon slices

Peanut butter, sliced bananas tossed with brown sugar and lemon juice, sliced turkey, lettuce, and crisply cooked bacon slices

Peanut butter, sliced bananas, granola, and
     crumbled bacon
and, last but not least, Elvis's favorite:
Peanut butter and mashed banana, on bread
     that's cooked in bacon fat and served with a
     glass of buttermilk. (It's up to you when you eat
     the bacon.)

# WHILE-WE'RE-AT-IT VARIATIONS

**In the cyber world, chat rooms are full of bacon-lovin' sandwich snackers who find all kinds of interesting ways to combine 2 pieces of bread and cooked bacon. Here's a sampling to help you get your search engine started:**

Egg salad with horseradish, caraway seeds,
     and crumbled bacon
Tuna salad with bean sprouts, tomato slices, lettuce,
     and crumbled bacon
Cream cheese mixed with chopped pecans, crushed
     pineapple, and crumbled bacon
Mayonnaise mixed with ample amounts of sliced green
     onions and crumbled bacon
Sourdough bread, avocado slices, tomato slices,
     grated Cheddar cheese, and crisply cooked
     bacon slices
Buttered bread, chopped pickled beets
     (with or without onions), and crisply cooked
     bacon slices

# Schmidty's Meat Loaf with Biscuits Instead

**When my friend Ron Schmidt went off to college, his mother gave him a binder filled with her handwritten recipes of his favorite dishes. He kept it his whole life, and often he or his wife, Ede, would refer to its well-worn pages. When I asked for his favorite recipe, Ron flipped to the meat loaf page in a heartbeat. He served his with mashed potatoes and I did, too, until my family tasted these buttermilk biscuits. After that, it was always "biscuits instead." You'll discover why.**

### SERVES 6 TO 8

| | |
|---|---|
| 3 | thick bacon slices (3 ounces uncooked), cut crosswise in half |
| 1 | medium onion, finely chopped |
| 3 | cloves garlic, minced |
| 2 | pounds ground lean beef |
| 1 | pound ground sausage meat, such as Jimmy Dean or ground pork |
| 1 | cup fine dry bread or cracker crumbs |
| 1/4 | cup ketchup |
| 1 | tablespoon Dijon mustard |
| 2 | eggs lightly beaten |
| 3 | dried bay leaves |

Biscuits Instead (recipe follows)

**PREHEAT** the oven to 350°F.

**IN A MEDIUM HEAVY SKILLET,** place the bacon slices in a single layer and cook over low to medium-low heat, turning as needed until limp and barely half-cooked. Transfer to a paper towel to drain. Pour off the bacon drippings, reserving 2 tablespoons in the skillet.

**IN THE SAME SKILLET,** add the onion and sauté over medium heat until translucent, 3 to 4 minutes. Stir in the garlic and cook until the garlic is lightly browned, 1 to 2 minutes. Remove with a slotted spoon to a large bowl.

**ADD THE GROUND BEEF,** sausage, bread crumbs, ketchup, and mustard to the bowl with the onion and garlic. Using 2 forks, rake and toss the mixture until combined. Add the beaten eggs and blend again. The mixture will be quite moist. Transfer to a 9-by-13-inch baking pan and gently form into a rectangular shape. Place the bay leaves on top and bake for 30 minutes.

**REMOVE THE MEAT LOAF** from the oven and arrange the half-cooked bacon slices along the top in diagonal stripes. Return to the oven and continue to bake for about 40 minutes longer, or until an instant-read thermometer inserted into the middle reads 165°F. Using 2 spatulas, lift the meat loaf out of the pan and onto a serving platter. Let rest for 10 minutes before serving. Pass the warm Biscuits Instead.

# BISCUITS INSTEAD

At Mother's Bistro & Bar in Portland, Oregon, pastry chef Debbie Putnam prepares hearty buttermilk and cream biscuits that are different from any others. Her recipe makes a very wet dough. In fact, you need to scoop, not cut, the dough in order to divide it into individual biscuits. The same goes for my rendition. If, by luck, you have a leftover biscuit or two, they will keep well for a day. To rewarm, simply wrap the biscuits in aluminum foil and place them in a 350°F oven for a few minutes.

**MAKES ABOUT 10 BISCUITS**

2    cups self-rising flour
$^1/_8$   teaspoon baking soda
$^3/_4$   teaspoon salt
2    tablespoons sugar
4    tablespoons cold unsalted butter, cut into small pieces
$^3/_4$   cup buttermilk
$^1/_2$   cup heavy (whipping) cream
1    cup all-purpose flour
2    tablespoons unsalted butter, melted (optional)

**PREHEAT** the oven to 500°F. Spray an 8-inch round glass cake pan with vegetable-oil cooking spray.

**IN A MIXING BOWL,** whisk together the self-rising flour, baking soda, salt, and sugar. Add the cold butter. Using a pastry blender, 2 knives, or your fingertips, work the mixture together until the butter is the size of peas. Stir in the buttermilk and cream and let the dough stand for 2 minutes. It will be sticky and wet.

**PLACE THE ALL-PURPOSE FLOUR** in another mixing bowl. Flour your hands well. Scoop or spoon a medium lemon–sized lump of wet dough into the flour to coat. Pick it up and gently shape it into a soft round. Shake off the excess flour and place it in the pan. Repeat with the remaining dough, placing the biscuits against each other, 8 around the edge and 2 in the center.

**BAKE THE BISCUITS** for 5 minutes. Reduce the oven temperature to 475°F and continue to bake until the biscuits are very brown, about 17 minutes longer. Remove from the oven and brush with the melted butter, if desired. Cool for 5 minutes before inverting the pan and removing the biscuits. Gently pull the biscuits apart and serve.

# Coq au Vin

This richly flavored stew is my version of the classic French dish in which chicken is braised with onions, thyme, smoky bacon, and red wine. I like to use a fruity California Zinfandel, along with a dash of cognac. I know what you're thinking: It's hard to pour expensive wine into a stew, but you'll discover it makes a difference with every bite.

As with most stews, if there's time, make it a day ahead to let the flavors develop.

**SERVES 4**

| | |
|---|---|
| 4 | tablespoons unsalted butter |
| 1 | chicken (3 to 3¹/₂ pounds), trimmed of fat and cut into 8 serving pieces |
| 5 | thick smoked bacon slices (5 ounces uncooked), coarsely chopped |
| 20 | small pearl onions (about 8 ounces), peeled |
| 3 | cloves garlic, minced |
| 1 | cup low- or no-sodium chicken broth |
| 1 | cup red wine |
| 2 | tablespoons cognac or brandy |
| 2 | tablespoons tomato paste |
| 1¹/₂ to 2 | teaspoons dried thyme |
| ¹/₂ | pound fresh small mushrooms, whole or sliced |
| 2 | tablespoons all-purpose flour |
| 3 | tablespoons chopped fresh flat-leaf parsley |

Coarse (kosher) salt and freshly ground pepper

**IN A LARGE SKILLET** or Dutch oven, melt 2 tablespoons of the butter over medium heat. Add the chicken in a single layer and fry until lightly browned, 7 to 10 minutes total. Transfer the chicken to a platter. Pour off the drippings, reserving 1 tablespoon in the skillet.

**IN THE SAME SKILLET,** add the bacon and onions and sauté over medium heat, stirring frequently, until the onions begin to brown, about 10 minutes. Add the garlic and sauté for 1 minute. Stir in the chicken broth, wine, cognac, tomato paste, and thyme. Return the chicken to the skillet and bring the mixture to a boil. Cover, reduce the heat to a simmer, and cook until the chicken is fork-tender, about 30 minutes.

**WITH A SLOTTED SPOON,** remove the chicken to a clean platter. Add the mushrooms to the skillet and simmer for 10 minutes. Meanwhile, in a small bowl, blend together the flour and the remaining 2 tablespoons butter to form a paste. Add the paste to the cooking liquid, stirring until thickened, 1 to 2 minutes.

**RETURN THE CHICKEN** to the skillet and simmer for 5 minutes longer. To serve, transfer the chicken and most of the onions and mushrooms to a warm platter (don't worry if some strays get left behind). Stir the sauce, pour it over the chicken, onions, and mushrooms, and garnish with chopped parsley. Or, simply serve from the skillet. At the table, season with salt and pepper to taste.

**IF MAKING AHEAD,** cool, cover, and refrigerate for up to 3 days. To reheat, preheat the oven to 350°F. Arrange the chicken in an ovenproof casserole, cover with the sauce, and bake until the meat is hot, 30 to 40 minutes.

# Not-Quite-Kosher Chopped Chicken Livers

Forget the schmaltz. This not-quite-traditional recipe forgoes the chicken fat and uses the smoky, rich taste and drippings from bacon for flavor. Suzy Kitman, an Oregon caterer and portrait painter, passed the recipe along to me from her mother, Carol Kitman, who described the spread as an ecumenical culinary marriage. Suzy's parents grew up in traditional Jewish families. As newlyweds, the young couple moved to Manhattan and a diverse ethnic neighborhood. Before long, they were eating things they had never heard of before. Along the way, somebody somewhere slipped in the bacon.

**SERVES 8 TO 10**

3   thick smoked bacon slices (3 ounces uncooked),
    cut crosswise into 1-inch pieces
1   large onion, cut into $^1/_4$-inch dice (about $1^1/_2$ cups)
1   pound chicken livers, trimmed of fat
2   hard-cooked eggs
Coarse (kosher) salt and freshly ground pepper
Handful of fresh flat-leaf parsley sprigs, trimmed
    and chopped
Waverly crackers or matzo for serving

**IN A MEDIUM HEAVY SKILLET,** cook the bacon pieces over low to medium-low heat, turning as needed to achieve uniform crispness. Using a slotted spoon, transfer to a paper towel to drain. Pour off the bacon drippings, reserving 2 tablespoons in the skillet. Coarsely chop the bacon and set aside.

**IN THE SAME SKILLET,** add the onion and sauté over medium-high heat until light brown with dark edges, about 5 minutes. With a slotted spoon, remove the onion to a medium bowl. In the same skillet, cook the chicken livers over high heat until browned but not dry or burned, about 10 minutes. Remove from the heat, cool, and coarsely chop the livers along with the eggs.

**TRANSFER** all ingredients to a bowl, and season with salt and pepper to taste. Cover with plastic wrap and chill for several hours or overnight. To serve, spoon the chopped chicken livers into an attractive bowl, garnish with parsley, and accompany with crackers or matzo.

# Bacon-Wrapped Filet Mignon with Maker's Mark Peppercorn Sauce

**Here is a special-occasion dish to beat all others. Great meat (as in bacon and filet). Great sauce (as in Kentucky bourbon). Great taste (as in take your first bite). Searing the bacon-wrapped filets in a cast-iron skillet leaves all those tasty bits in the pan, ready to season the intensely flavorful and peppery sauce. It's the kind of sauce you pass, and a little goes a long way. This is not a dish for wimps.**

**SERVES 2**

4   tablespoons olive oil
1   teaspoon dried marjoram, crumbled
1   teaspoon coarse (kosher) salt
2   beef tenderloin filets, each 6 to 8 ounces and
    1 1/2 to 2 inches thick
2   regular or thick pepper bacon slices
    (1 1/2 to 2 ounces uncooked)
3   cloves garlic, minced
1   tablespoon aged balsamic vinegar
1 1/2 teaspoons cracked or coarsely ground pepper
2   cups low-sodium beef broth
1   tablespoon Maker's Mark Kentucky bourbon

**IN A CUP OR SMALL BOWL,** mix together 2 tablespoons of the olive oil, the marjoram, and salt. Rub the mixture over the filets. Wrap each filet with a slice of bacon and secure with 1 or 2 toothpicks. Place the filets in a shallow pan, cover with plastic wrap, and marinate for 1 hour at room temperature.

**IN A MEDIUM HEAVY SAUCEPAN,** combine the garlic, vinegar, and pepper and boil over medium-high heat until almost no liquid remains, about 1 minute. Add the broth and continue to boil until the liquid is reduced to 1/2 cup, about 20 minutes. Set aside.

**PREHEAT** the oven to 350°F.

**IN A MEDIUM CAST-IRON SKILLET,** heat the remaining 2 tablespoons olive oil over medium-high heat for 1 minute. Fry the filets for 4 minutes per side. To sear the edges, use tongs to hold and rotate the filets' bacon-wrapped edges against the skillet for 1 minute.

**PLACE THE SKILLET** and filets in the oven. For medium-rare, bake for 15 minutes or until an instant-read thermometer reads 130°F to 135°F. Using a pot holder to hold the skillet's hot handle, remove from the oven. Transfer the filets to a platter and let them rest for 5 to 7 minutes so the meat juices can redistribute and the residual heat can finish cooking the filets (135°F to 140°F). Remove the toothpicks.

**MEANWHILE,** pour off the skillet drippings, reserving about 2 teaspoons in the skillet. Add the pepper sauce and bring to a boil, stirring constantly to scrape up the browned bits from the bottom. Stir in the bourbon and simmer for 15 to 30 seconds. Pour the sauce into a small pitcher. Serve the filets, passing the sauce.

# GREAT PARTY WRAP-UPS

Playing dress-up with bacon

# Seared Sea Scallops Wrapped in Bacon with Celery Root Purée

Chef Kenny Giambalvo serves this elegant first course at Bluehour, his restaurant in Portland, Oregon. It's such a favorite that his customers make a point of telling him he can't ever take it off the menu or tinker with it in any way. No wonder. Kenny keeps each ingredient's personality evident in every bite while creating the perfect balance of textures and flavors. It's dreamy.

Celery root, also known as celeriac, is a kissing cousin of stalk celery, but it is grown for its dense, fleshy root and subtle celery flavor. It can be served raw in salads or cooked in soups, stews, and purées. Once the root is peeled, you'll need to use it right away or it discolors. If you decide to prepare it ahead of time for this purée, submerge the peeled root in water with a bit of lemon juice.

12   large fresh sea scallops (12 to 14 ounces total), small tough muscles removed

6   thin or regular smoked bacon slices ($2\frac{1}{2}$ to $3\frac{1}{2}$ ounces uncooked), cut crosswise in half

1   large celery root (about 1 pound), peeled and cut into small chunks

About 1 cup heavy (whipping) cream, heated

Coarse (kosher) salt and freshly ground pepper

Pinch of nutmeg

1   cup vegetable broth

Juice of 1 lemon

$\frac{3}{4}$   cup ($1\frac{1}{2}$ sticks) unsalted butter, cut into pieces

5   tablespoons olive oil

$\frac{1}{4}$   cup nonpareil capers

All-purpose flour for dredging

$\frac{1}{2}$   bunch fresh flat-leaf parsley, leaves picked and finely chopped

**WRAP EACH SCALLOP** in a piece of bacon one and a half wraps, from bottom to top to bottom, trimming off any excess. It is not necessary to secure the bacon with toothpicks. Set aside in a pan, cover loosely with plastic wrap, and chill while preparing the celery root.

**IN A SAUCEPAN,** cover the celery root with water. Bring to a simmer over medium-high heat and cook until tender, about 20 minutes. Drain off the water and return the pan with the celery root to medium heat. Continue to briefly cook the celery root, stirring constantly with a wooden spoon, until all the water has evaporated.

**WHILE THE CELERY ROOT** is still hot, run it through a food mill, ricer, or food processor. Add enough hot cream to reach a creamy consistency. Season with salt, pepper, and nutmeg to taste. To keep the purée warm, spoon it into the top pan of a double boiler over simmering water.

**MEANWHILE,** in a saucepan, bring the vegetable broth to a simmer over medium-high heat. Add the lemon juice and whisk in the butter. When the butter is blended, bring the sauce just to a boil. Remove from heat, and adjust the seasonings with salt and pepper. Cover to keep warm and set aside.

**IN A SAUTÉ PAN,** heat 2 tablespoons of the olive oil over medium-high heat. Quickly dredge the capers in flour, shaking off any excess. Fry the capers until lightly browned and crispy, about 1 minute. Using a slotted spoon, transfer to a paper towel to drain.

**IN THE SAME SAUTÉ PAN,** heat the remaining 3 tablespoons olive oil. Season the scallops with salt and pepper. Using tongs, sear the scallops on all sides, starting with the bottom, until the bacon is golden brown and crisp, about 4 minutes.

**TO SERVE,** spoon the celery root purée in the middle of 4 plates, dividing equally. Place 3 scallops on each plate. Spoon a little sauce around the scallops. Garnish with chopped parsley and fried capers and serve immediately.

# Do-You-Remember-When Wrapped Bacon Treats

**We've all tasted, seen, or heard about one or more of these yummy excuses for eating bacon with a cocktail napkin. Each treat requires only a few ingredients and even fewer instructions. So wrap 'em up, broil them all over, and pass one on to me.**

**WRAP A FRESHLY SHUCKED OYSTER** in partially cooked bacon, and secure with a short, fancy skewer or toothpick. Broil or bake in a 450°F oven until the bacon is crisp. Serve as is, or remove the skewer and serve on toast points. That's your **ANGEL ON HORSE-BACK**. Add some brimstone and fire, a.k.a. Tabasco sauce, and it becomes a **DEVIL ON HORSEBACK**.

**STUFF A LARGE PITTED ITALIAN PRUNE** with roasted almond and mango chutney, wrap in partially cooked bacon, and secure with a short, fancy skewer or toothpick. Broil or bake in a 450°F oven until the bacon is crisp. Serve as is, or remove the skewer and serve on toast points. That's the British version of a devil on horseback.

**WRAP YOUR FAVORITE STUFFED GIANT OLIVE** in partially cooked bacon, and secure with a short, fancy skewer or toothpick. Broil or bake in a 450°F oven until the bacon is crisp. (Be adventurous; besides pimento, there are jalapeño-, garlic-, and caper-stuffed olives.)

**WRAP A BITE-SIZED PIECE OF CHICKEN** and a slice or small chunk of crystallized ginger in partially cooked bacon, and secure with a short, fancy skewer or toothpick. Broil or bake in a 450°F oven until the bacon is crisp.

**WRAP A BITE-SIZED PIECE OF PINEAPPLE** in partially cooked bacon, and secure with a short, fancy skewer or toothpick. Broil or bake in a 450°F oven until the bacon is crisp. Add a bite-sized slice of green bell pepper as a variation.

**WRAP TINY HOT DOGS OR COOKED SAUSAGES** in partially cooked bacon, and secure with a manly toothpick. Broil or bake in a 450°F oven until the bacon is crisp, and pass the French's mustard.

**AND FINALLY,** from the days of poodle skirts and fuzzy dice, wrap a saltine cracker in partially cooked bacon, and secure with a toothpick. Broil or bake in a 450°F oven until the bacon is crisp.

101

# Halibut en Papillote

Great things come in small packages, especially when you cook *en papillote*, in parchment paper. This combines the techniques of baking, braising, and steaming, and seals in the flavors of the ingredients you are using. It's also very easy to do.

In this recipe, bacon is used as a smoky and salty seasoning. It gives a delicious finish to the natural juices of the delicate halibut, sweet tomatoes, and onions. For a delightful surprise, I like to tuck some tiny heart-shaped carrot slices inside the packets.

**SERVES 4**

4   12-inch square sheets parchment paper
2   thick smoked bacon slices (2 ounces uncooked), cut crosswise into 1/4-inch pieces
4   halibut fillets, each about 6 ounces and 3/4 inch thick
2   medium tomatoes, cored and cut into 1/2-inch pieces
1   sweet white onion, thinly sliced
16  heart-shaped carrot slices (optional) (see Note)
2   teaspoons dried tarragon
Coarse (kosher) salt and freshly ground pepper
4   tablespoons dry white wine
1   egg white, beaten

**PREHEAT** the oven to 350°F. Fold each sheet of parchment paper in half.

**IN A MEDIUM HEAVY SKILLET,** cook the bacon pieces over low to medium-low heat, turning as needed to achieve uniform crispness. Using a slotted spoon, transfer to a paper towel to drain.

**ARRANGE A FILLET** to one side of the fold line of each parchment sheet. Divide and arrange the tomato pieces, onion slices, and carrot hearts, if desired, on the top and sides of each fillet. Sprinkle the fillets with the tarragon, bacon pieces, and salt and pepper. Drizzle 1 tablespoon white wine over each fillet.

**LIGHTLY BRUSH** the inside edges of each parchment packet with egg white. Beginning with a folded corner, twist and fold the edges of each packet together. Arrange the packets on a baking sheet and bake for 20 minutes. The packets will puff up. Place the unopened packets on plates and let diners cut open at the table.

 **Note:** To make carrot hearts, slice 1 or 2 medium carrots into rounds about 1/4-inch thick. Arrange the slices on a cutting board. Using a heart-shaped garnish cutter that is slightly smaller in diameter than the carrot slices, cut each slice into a heart.

## Variation:

# FOR SEA SCALLOPS EN PAPILLOTE,

follow the recipe above, using 12 fresh sea scallops (12 to 14 ounces total). Arrange 3 scallops on each parchment square and proceed as directed.

# Bacon-Wrapped Zucchini Flans

As a first course or alongside the entrée, these individual zucchini flans wrapped in bacon add an elegant touch to a dinner party. You'll find the lemon zest provides just the right seasoning for the silky cheese custard, and the bacon brings it all together. When choosing the bacon, look for lean, straight slices.

**SERVES 6**

1 1/2 pounds zucchini

1    teaspoon salt

12   regular bacon slices (6 3/4 ounces uncooked)

2    eggs

2    tablespoons all-purpose flour

1/4  cup grated Parmigiano-Reggiano cheese

1/4  cup heavy (whipping) cream

2    teaspoons grated lemon zest

1    teaspoon dried basil

Coarse (kosher) salt and freshly ground pepper

**PREHEAT** the oven to 375°F. Set aside 2 rimmed baking sheets; leave 1 ungreased, and line the other with parchment paper and grease with butter. Make sure the parchment-lined pan is flat and not warped.

**WITH A SHARP KNIFE,** cut each zucchini into long diagonal slices. Stack 2 or 3 slices—no more—and hold them in place with the fingers of one hand. Cut the slices into julienne strips as wide as they are thick. (This also can be done in a food processor fitted with a julienne slicer.) Place the zucchini strips in a colander, set in the sink, and sprinkle with the salt. Let stand for 30 minutes.

**PLACE THE BACON SLICES** on the ungreased baking sheet and bake until slightly brown, 10 to 12 minutes. Transfer to a paper towel to drain. While the slices are still warm and pliable, use them to line six 3-inch round muffin or cookie cutters, 2 for each cutter. Then place the cutters on the parchment-lined baking sheet.

**IN A LARGE MIXING BOWL,** beat the eggs, flour, cheese, cream, lemon zest, basil, and salt and pepper to taste. Squeeze the zucchini strips between paper towels and add them to the egg mixture. Stir until well blended.

**DIVIDE THE ZUCCHINI-EGG MIXTURE** among the bacon-lined muffin cutters. Bake until set, 25 minutes. Remove from the oven and gently unmold on a serving plate.

104

# Grilled Shrimp Wrapped in Bacon

**I have yet to fix these shrimp and ever have any left over. Could it be my cooking? I wish I could say it was.**

**MAKES 13 TO 15**

<sup>1</sup>/<sub>2</sub>    cup olive oil or vegetable oil

2      tablespoons white wine vinegar

1<sup>1</sup>/<sub>2</sub>    teaspoons Dijon mustard

1      tablespoon chopped fresh dill

Coarse (kosher) salt and freshly ground pepper

1      pound jumbo shrimp (13 to 15 per pound),
       peeled and deveined, with tails intact

5      regular lean bacon slices (about 2<sup>3</sup>/<sub>4</sub> ounces
       uncooked), cut crosswise into thirds

Fresh watercress for garnishing

**IN A SMALL BOWL,** whisk together the olive oil, vinegar, mustard, and dill. Season with salt and pepper to taste.

**IN A MEDIUM NONREACTIVE BOWL,** pour the marinade over the shrimp and toss. Cover, chill, and marinate for several hours, tossing several times.

**PREHEAT** a gas or charcoal grill. (*Note:* A charcoal grill will be at the right temperature when you can place your hand over the white-ashed coals, about 1 inch from the grate, and count to three, using the "one-one-thousand" style.) Just before grilling the shrimp, wipe the grate from back to front with a clean rag dipped in vegetable oil. If you go from front to back, you might lose some hair on your arm.

**DRAIN THE SHRIMP.** Wrap a piece of bacon around each shrimp, and secure with a short skewer or tooth-pick. Grill until the bacon is crisp and the shrimp is cooked, about 4 minutes per side. You can also grill the shrimp under a preheated broiler, 5 inches from the heat, for 4 to 5 minutes per side. Watch carefully to prevent the bacon from burning. Remove from heat and arrange on a large platter. Garnish with water-cress. Serve either skewered or unskewered.

# Fresh Figs with Bacon and Goat Cheese

Where I live in Oregon, little green figs grow in the neighborhood. They have a pinkish blush and a luscious sweetness. Known as white, or Calimyrna, figs, these bite-sized gems make a divine pop-in-your-mouth snack and, as you'll discover, an hors d'oeuvre that is hard to resist.

In most specialty produce markets, fresh figs are available year-round and peak from mid-August through October. If you can't find Calimyrna figs, substitute small, fresh Black Mission or Brown Turkey figs. When it comes to the bacon, use a sweet, smoky bacon. I like Carlton Dry-Cured Bacon (see Sources, page 128, under The Grateful Palate), which is smoked over alderwood and comes from Oregon, too.

**MAKES 24**

4 to 6 regular smoked bacon slices (2$^1/_4$ to 3$^1/_2$
   ounces uncooked)
12  small fresh ripe green figs, such as white,
   or Calimyrna, halved lengthwise
About 1 tablespoon balsamic vinegar
$^1/_3$  cup (about 1$^1/_2$ ounces) crumbled mild herbed
   goat cheese

**PREHEAT** the oven to 350°F.

**IN A MEDIUM HEAVY SKILLET,** place the bacon slices in a single layer and cook over low to medium-low heat, turning as needed until just beginning to brown. Transfer to a paper towel to drain. Cut each bacon slice into 4 or 6 pieces.

**ARRANGE THE FIGS** on a baking sheet, cut-sides up. Brush the cut surfaces with balsamic vinegar. Place a piece of bacon on each cut side. Top with a small crumble of cheese. Bake until the figs are warmed, about 8 minutes. The cheese will not melt but may toast a bit. Serve immediately.

# "Bloody Mary, She Loves Bacon"

"Want to know how to wrap a bacon lover around your little finger?" she asked. "Serve them a good Bloody Mary and forget about rumaki and angels on horseback. Give them a taste of this."

There on a little silver tray were glistening, caramelized pieces of bacon basking on beet rounds, each one tastier than the last—or so it seemed. The grainy mustard-brown sugar glaze proved the perfect foil for the tart and tangy Bloody Mary. The golden beet slices act as little edible plates, making it easier to go back for seconds, thirds, and fourths.

**MAKES 4 DRINKS AND 16 TO 20 BACON BITES**

### GLAZED BACON:

| | |
|---|---|
| 1/2 | cup firmly packed light brown sugar |
| 1/2 | teaspoon grated orange zest |
| 2 | tablespoons fresh orange juice |
| 1 | tablespoon grainy mustard |
| 4 | thick, meaty uniform bacon slices (4 ounces uncooked) |
| 2 | small to medium golden beets |

Celery leaves for garnishing (optional)

### BLOODY MARYS:

| | |
|---|---|
| 2 | cups canned tomato juice |
| 4 | tablespoons Worcestershire sauce |
| 1/2 | teaspoon Tabasco sauce |
| 3 | teaspoons cream-style prepared horseradish |
| 1/2 | teaspoon fresh lemon juice |
| 1/2 | teaspoon dried dill |
| 1/2 | teaspoon celery salt |
| 1 | teaspoon freshly ground black pepper |
| 1/4 | teaspoon white pepper |
| 1 | lime or lemon, cut into 6 to 8 wedges |

Saucer of salt for coating rims of glasses

Ice cubes for serving

| | |
|---|---|
| 3/4 | cup (6 ounces) premium vodka |
| 4 | lemon or lime wedges for garnishing |
| 4 | thin celery stalk tops for garnishing |

**TO MAKE THE GLAZED BACON:** Preheat the oven to 350°F. Line a rimmed baking sheet with aluminum foil.

**IN A SMALL BOWL,** whisk together the sugar, orange zest, orange juice, and mustard.

**PLACE THE BACON SLICES** on the baking sheet in a single layer so they are not touching. Using a spoon, liberally spread the glaze over the bacon slices, about 1 1/2 teaspoons per slice. Bake until the bacon fat browns, about 12 minutes. Remove from oven. Using tongs or a fork, turn the bacon over. Liberally spread the glaze over the slices. Return to the oven and bake until browned, shiny, and caramelized, 12 to 14 minutes. Watch carefully; baking times will vary depending on the bacon's thickness. Let the bacon cool to the touch.

**TRIM, PEEL, AND CUT** the beets into 1/8-inch slices. Cut or break the bacon slices into pieces that will cover but not overlap the beet slices. Dab a bit of bacon glaze in the center of each beet slice and place a bacon piece on top. Garnish with a tiny leaf from a celery stalk, if desired. Arrange on a tray and serve with Bloody Marys.

**TO MAKE THE BLOODY MARYS:** In a pitcher, whisk or stir together the tomato juice, Worcestershire sauce, Tabasco sauce, horseradish, lemon juice, dill, celery salt, black pepper, and white pepper.

**RUB A LIME WEDGE** around the rims of 4 double old-fashioned glasses, bucket glasses, or any glasses with a 1 1/2-cup volume. Dip and rotate the rims in the saucer of salt, making sure to keep the salt on the outside. Fill each glass with ice cubes. Pour 1 1/2 ounces vodka into each glass. Add 1/2 cup tomato juice mixture to each glass. Garnish with a lemon wedge and a thin celery stalk.

# Arlene's Rumaki

Arlene's rumaki never makes it out of the kitchen when we all get together. She's getting the dinner ready, I'm making the salad, and everyone else is doing their bit. Then Arlene brings the rumaki out of the fridge and sticks them under the broiler. We keep thinking, we'll sit out in the living room with a cool martini or a glass of beer, but it's much more fun to eat these hot niblets right off the broiler pan.

## MAKES 16

- ¹/₄   cup soy sauce
- 2     tablespoons vegetable oil
- ¹/₂   teaspoon grated fresh ginger or 1 teaspoon ground ginger
- 1     clove garlic, finely minced
- ¹/₂   teaspoon curry powder
- ¹/₂   pound fresh chicken livers, cut in half or into bite-sized pieces
- 8     regular lean bacon slices (4 ounces uncooked)
- 8     water chestnuts, cut in half or into slices

**PREHEAT** the broiler.

**IN A SMALL BOWL,** whisk together the soy sauce, oil, ginger, garlic, and curry. Add the chicken livers. Cover and chill for 1 hour.

**IN A MEDIUM HEAVY SKILLET,** place the bacon slices in a single layer and cook over low to medium-low heat, turning as needed until just beginning to brown. Transfer to a paper towel to drain. Cut the bacon slices crosswise so each one is large enough to fit around a piece of liver and water chestnut.

**DRAIN THE CHICKEN LIVERS.** Wrap a piece of liver and a piece of water chestnut in a bacon slice, and secure with a toothpick. Arrange the wrapped chicken livers on the lid of a broiler pan and broil, turning once, until the bacon is crisp, about 5 minutes.

# LIVIN' HIGH ON THE HOG

Unexpected treats for a bacon-lover's sweet tooth

# Try-It-You'll-Like-It Bacon Brittle

This is one of those times you don't tell your friends exactly what you've got up your sleeve—or in the candy box. You just say, "Here's the best homemade brittle you'll ever taste. Betcha can't eat just one piece." That's all it will take.

**MAKES ABOUT 1 POUND**

1    cup sugar

$^1/_2$  cup light corn syrup

$^1/_2$  cup water

1    tablespoon unsalted butter

2    teaspoons vanilla extract

1    teaspoon baking soda

$^1/_2$  cup (about 2 ounces) chopped pecans

$^1/_3$ to $^1/_2$ cup cooked bacon bits (6 to 8 ounces uncooked)

**GREASE OR BUTTER** a large nonstick baking sheet.

**IN A MEDIUM HEAVY SAUCEPAN,** combine the sugar, corn syrup, and water over medium heat. Stir until the sugar dissolves and the syrup comes to a boil. Attach a candy thermometer to the pan. Increase the heat to high and cook, without stirring, until the mixture reaches 290°F. Immediately remove from heat.

**STIR IN THE BUTTER,** vanilla, baking soda, pecans, and bacon bits. Watch out, the mixture will foam. When the foam subsides, pour the hot mixture onto the prepared baking sheet as thinly as possible. Do not use a spatula. Cool for at least 10 minutes before breaking into pieces. Store in a covered container for as long as it lasts. (Not long enough.)

# Double-Crunch Peanut Butter Cookies

This is everything a cookie should be—crunchy, soft, sweet, and chewy—and it's also loaded with crushed bacon brittle. It's incredibly good. Got milk?

No bacon brittle? For a quick substitute, combine 2 tablespoons of cooked bacon pieces with 1 cup crushed store-bought peanut brittle. While it's not exactly the same, it will do the trick.

**MAKES ABOUT TWENTY 4-INCH COOKIES**

2$\frac{1}{4}$ cups all-purpose flour

2  teaspoons baking soda

$\frac{1}{4}$  teaspoon of salt

$\frac{1}{2}$  cup (1 stick) unsalted butter at room temperature

$\frac{1}{2}$  cup shortening

1  cup firmly packed dark brown sugar

1  cup granulated sugar

$\frac{2}{3}$  cup chunky or creamy peanut butter

1  egg

1$\frac{1}{2}$ teaspoons vanilla extract

1$\frac{1}{2}$ cups chopped Try-It-You'll-Like-It Bacon Brittle (page 114)

1$\frac{1}{2}$ cups (8 ounces) peanut butter chips

**PREHEAT** the oven to 350°F. Line 2 baking sheets with parchment paper or grease them. (Since the brittle bits sometimes stick, I prefer using parchment paper.)

**IN A LARGE MIXING BOWL,** whisk together the flour, baking soda, and salt. Set aside.

**IN AN ELECTRIC MIXTURE,** beat the butter, shortening, brown sugar, and granulated sugar on medium until smooth. Add the peanut butter and beat until smooth. Add the egg and beat until smooth. Beat in the vanilla, then beat in the flour mixture, scraping the sides of the bowl. Stir in the brittle and the peanut butter chips.

**ROLL THE DOUGH** into golf ball–sized balls, using 2 tablespoons dough for each ball. Arrange the balls at least 3$\frac{1}{2}$ inches apart on the prepared baking sheets. Flatten each cookie with your fingers to form a 3 inch cookie, or with a fork, making a crisscross design (dipping the fork in ice water prevents it from sticking to the dough). Bake until the cookies are golden, about 14 minutes for soft cookies, about 16 minutes for crisp cookies. Let the cookies cool for 2 minutes, then transfer to a wire rack, or slide the parchment from the sheet to the rack.

# Pear-Apple Crisp with Brown Sugar–Bacon Topping

Crisps are such easy, flavorful desserts, and this sophisticated version is no exception. With its apple brandy-plumped raisins and brown sugar–bacon topping, it's simply out of this world. When you are ready to serve, pass a pitcher of heavy cream or top each portion with a scoop of softened French vanilla ice cream.

SERVES 6

**FILLING:**

1   cup golden raisins

3   tablespoons apple or pear brandy

1   tablespoon Grand Marnier (optional)

4   medium apples, such as Braeburn, peeled, cored, and cut into 1/4-inch slices

1/2   teaspoon ground cinnamon

6   tablespoons granulated sugar

3   small pears, such as Comice, peeled, cored, and cut into 1/4-inch slices

**TOPPING:**

8 to 12 thick bacon slices (8 to 12 ounces uncooked), cut crosswise into 1-inch pieces

1/2   cup firmly packed light brown sugar

1/2   cup all-purpose flour

4   tablespoons granulated sugar

1/2   cup (1 stick) unsalted butter, cut into pieces

3/4   cup (about 3 ounces) toasted hazelnuts or pecans (see Note)

Heavy (whipping) cream or softened French vanilla ice cream for serving

**PREHEAT** the oven to 350°F. Butter an 8-by-8-by-2-inch baking pan.

**TO MAKE THE FILLING:** In a small bowl, combine the raisins, brandy, and Grand Marnier, if using. Let stand for 30 minutes, or microwave for 30 seconds and let stand for 15 minutes.

**IN A MEDIUM SAUCEPAN,** combine the apples, cinnamon, and sugar over medium heat. Bring the mixture to a boil. Reduce the heat to medium-low and simmer, stirring frequently, until the apples are tender, about 5 minutes.

**REMOVE FROM HEAT** and transfer to a large bowl. Add the pears and raisins with their soaking liquid and stir gently. Transfer the mixture to the prepared pan.

**TO MAKE THE TOPPING:** In a medium heavy skillet, cook the bacon pieces over low to medium-low heat, turning as needed to achieve uniform crispness. Using a slotted spoon, transfer to a paper towel to drain. Pour off the bacon drippings, but don't wipe or clean the skillet. Return the bacon to the pan. Sprinkle 4 tablespoons of the brown sugar over the bacon and cook over medium-low heat until the sugar is no longer granular and has coated the bacon pieces, about 2 minutes. Using a slotted spoon, transfer to a paper towel. Chop the bacon into bits.

**IN A MEDIUM BOWL,** mix together the flour, granulated sugar, and the remaining 4 tablespoons brown sugar. Add the butter and mix together with a fork until crumbly. Stir in the hazelnuts and half of the bacon bits. Sprinkle the topping over the apple mixture. Sprinkle the remaining bacon bits over the topping.

**BAKE UNTIL THE TOP IS LIGHTLY BROWNED,** about 35 minutes. Let cool slightly on a wire rack before serving. Serve warm, and pass a pitcher of cream or serve with softened French vanilla ice cream.

Note: **To toast hazelnuts,** preheat the oven to 350°F. Spread the nuts on a rimmed baking sheet and bake, stirring occasionally, until the skins crack and the nuts brown, 10 to 15 minutes. Wrap the nuts in a kitchen towel and let "steam" for 5 minutes. Rub the towel briskly between your hands, which will cause most of the skins to flake off. **To toast pecans,** preheat the oven to 350°F. Spread the nuts on a rimmed baking sheet and bake, stirring occasionally, until brown, 10 to 15 minutes.

# Hazelnut-Bacon Candy Crunch

**Have a sweet tooth? Like nuts? Love bacon? What are you waiting for?**

**MAKES 1 CUP**

1    tablespoon pure maple syrup

1    teaspoon vanilla extract

1    tablespoon firmly packed light or dark brown sugar

2    tablespoons granulated sugar

2    teaspoons vegetable oil

$^3/_4$    cup (about 3 ounces) toasted hazelnuts (see Note, page 118)

$^1/_4$ to $^1/_3$ cup cooked bacon bits (4 to 6 ounces uncooked)

$^1/_2$    teaspoon ground cinnamon

**PREHEAT** the oven or toaster oven to 350°F.

**IN A SMALL SAUCEPAN,** combine the maple syrup, vanilla, brown sugar, 1 tablespoon of the granulated sugar, and the oil. Bring to a boil over medium heat, whisking constantly. Stir in the nuts and bacon bits, and continue to whisk until the nuts are shiny and glazed and the liquid is gone, about 2 minutes. Transfer the nut mixture to a small bowl.

**IN A CUP,** mix together the remaining 1 tablespoon granulated sugar and the cinnamon. Sprinkle the sugar mixture over the nuts and toss. Spread the coated nuts on a baking sheet and bake for about 4 minutes, watching to make sure the mixture doesn't burn. Remove from the oven and let cool. Refrigerate any leftovers in a covered container for up to 2 weeks.

# It's-Mine-You-Can't-Have-It Maple Sundae

I'm generous to a fault except when it comes to sundaes made with maple syrup and anything made with bacon. The combination of maple syrup and bacon is terrific. Have your doubts? You adore it for breakfast, why not dessert? (You can always add less bacon to the hazelnut crunch. After one try, you'll probably add more.)

6 tablespoons to $1/2$ cup pure maple syrup

4 scoops French vanilla ice cream

$1/3$ to $1/2$ cup Hazelnut-Bacon Candy Crunch (page 119)

$1/2$ cup lightly sweetened heavy (whipping) cream, whipped

2 maraschino cherries with stems

**IN EACH OF 2 DEEP STEMMED GLASSES,** pour 1 tablespoon of the maple syrup. Alternate the scoops of ice cream with spoonfuls of maple syrup, sprinkling each layer with 1 generous tablespoon of the crunch. Top with whipped cream and a maraschino cherry. Serve immediately.

120

# Ruby Raisin Mincemeat Tart with Mulled Wine Sorbet

If you love dried fruit and autumn spices *and* you're a bacon lover, you'll find any excuse to make this rustic tart. It goes together quickly. After dinner, serve it with a small scoop of mulled wine sorbet. In the morning, a sliver or slice with a cup of coffee is better than breakfast.

**SERVES 8**

**FILLING:**

5    thick bacon slices (5 ounces uncooked), coarsely chopped

1    cup (about 4 ounces) coarsely chopped mixed dried fruit, loosely packed (see Note)

3    tablespoons dried cranberries

2    tablespoons golden raisins

2    tablespoons firmly packed dark or light brown sugar

1    teaspoon grated lemon zest

1    teaspoon grated orange zest

1/4  teaspoon ground nutmeg

1/4  teaspoon ground allspice

2 to 3 tablespoons brandy

1/2  cup fresh orange juice

**CRUST:**

1 1/4 cups all-purpose flour

1/2  teaspoon salt

6    tablespoons frozen unsalted butter

2    tablespoons frozen lard or shortening (see Note)

4    tablespoons or more ice water

1    tablespoon granulated sugar

Mulled Wine Sorbet for serving (see page 124)

**TO MAKE THE FILLING:** In a 1-quart saucepan, combine the bacon, mixed dried fruit, cranberries, raisins, brown sugar, lemon zest, orange zest, nutmeg, allspice, brandy, and orange juice. Bring to a simmer over medium heat. Simmer, stirring frequently, until the liquid is reduced and thickened but the mixture is still moist and juicy, 3 to 4 minutes. Let cool.

**TO MAKE THE CRUST:** In a medium bowl, whisk together the flour and salt. (If time permits, chill the bowl and flour mixture for 30 minutes before using.) Using the large holes of a grater, grate the frozen butter and lard into the flour mixture. (The frozen fat is easier to incorporate into the dry ingredients and remains cold for a flakier crust. Using a pastry blender, 2 knives, or your fingertips, work the mixture together until it is crumbly. Sprinkle in the ice water, beginning with 3 tablespoons, and mix until the dough holds together when pressed. Shape into a disk, wrap in plastic wrap, and chill for 1 hour.

**PREHEAT** the oven to 375°F. Line a baking sheet with parchment paper.

**PLACE THE DOUGH** on a lightly floured surface and roll it into a 12-inch circle. (It doesn't have to be perfect.) Spread the filling on the dough, leaving a 1½-inch border. With moistened fingers, fold the uncovered dough up and over the filling to create pleats. Lightly press the pleats together. Dip a pastry brush in water, moisten the edges of the crust, and sprinkle with the granulated sugar.

**BAKE** until the crust is golden, about 30 minutes. (If the fruit begins to brown, cover it with aluminum foil.) Slip the parchment paper and tart onto a wire rack to cool. Serve warm or at room temperature with Mulled Wine Sorbet.

**Note:** Prepackaged mixed dried fruit is available in supermarkets. A premium brand typically comes in an 8-ounce package containing pitted prunes, dried apples, apricots, peaches, and pears.

**Lard** is made from rendered and clarified pork fat. It has the consistency of vegetable shortening and creates tender, flaky pastries. It is readily available in supermarkets in 1-pound packages. When tightly wrapped, lard will keep for up to 6 months at room temperature and even longer when chilled.

# MULLED WINE SORBET

Thanks go to Jennifer Welshhons, the creative chef at Wildwood Restaurant & Bar in Portland, Oregon, for this ruby-red sorbet. It's delicious with any wintertime pie. For the recipe, she uses three-fourths of a bottle of hearty Cabernet Sauvignon. "That way," she says, "you can make the sorbet and have enough left over to enjoy a glass."

**MAKES 1 QUART**

8 to 10 dried figs
$1/2$　cup dried cherries
1　apple, cored and coarsely chopped
1　pear, cored and coarsely chopped
$3/4$　bottle (562 ml, or about $2 1/4$ cups) Cabernet Sauvignon or Zinfandel
$1 1/2$ cups water
$1 1/2$ cups fresh orange juice
1　orange, zested into long strips
$1/2$　lemon, zested into long strips
2　cinnamon sticks
4　juniper berries
4　peppercorns
3　cloves
1　star anise (see Note)
Pinch of fennel seeds

**IN A LARGE SAUCEPAN,** combine the figs, cherries, apple, pear, $1/2$ bottle of the wine (375 ml, or about $1 1/2$ cups), the water, orange juice, orange zest, and lemon zest. Add the cinnamon sticks. In a 2-inch mesh tea ball or cheesecloth, combine the juniper berries, peppercorns, cloves, star anise, and fennel seeds and place in the pan. Bring the mixture to a boil over medium heat, reduce the heat to a simmer, and cook until the fruit is tender, about 45 minutes. Remove from heat and let cool.

**REMOVE THE TEA BALL.** Purée the mixture in batches in a blender and pass through a fine sieve. This will take time. While you can hasten the process by pressing on the saucelike purée, you'll extract more flavor if you let it strain slowly for several hours or overnight. (The fruit purée left in the strainer makes a tasty applesauce-like mixture.) Stir the remaining $1/4$ bottle of wine (187 ml, or about $3/4$ cup) into the strained liquid.

**CHILL THE MULLED WINE MIXTURE,** then freeze according to your ice cream maker's instructions. Since it contains alcohol, the sorbet will take longer to harden and will be a little softer than most sorbets.

 **Note:** Star anise can be found in Asian grocery stores, spice shops, and some supermarkets. The star-shaped spice has a sweet anise flavor.

# God's Little Acre Apple Hand Pies

For many of us, *God's Little Acre*, written by Erskine Caldwell, was our first flashlight-in-bed racy book. In the 1940s, Caldwell was literary America's "big apple," selling more books than any other writer in U.S. history. The man also liked apple pie. In 1937, when an aspiring cookbook author asked him for a recipe, he offered up a two-crusted apple pie that left out the filling altogether. The crust was a good one, made with shortening (for flakiness) and grated cheese (for flavor).

With poetic license and some culinary chutzpah, the original has been spruced up by adding flecks of savory bacon to the crust and creating a fresh apple filling. It also is divided into four hand pies, giving a greater crust-to-apple ratio. Trust me, you'll want as much of this crust as you can get.

**MAKES FOUR 6-INCH PIES**

**CRUST:**

2    cups all-purpose flour

$1/2$   teaspoon salt

$1/2$   teaspoon sugar

$1/2$   teaspoon baking powder

$2/3$   cup frozen lard or shortening (see Note, page 123)

2    tablespoons frozen unsalted butter

1    cup (4 ounces) grated sharp Cheddar cheese

4    tablespoons or more ice water

6    frozen thick bacon slices (6 ounces uncooked)

**FILLING:**

2    tablespoons unsalted butter

1    pound apples, such as Braeburn, peeled, cored, and cut into eighths

$1/2$   cup sugar

$1/2$   teaspoon ground cinnamon

Pinch of salt

1    teaspoon to 1 tablespoon fresh lemon juice

➥

125

**TO MAKE THE CRUST:** In a medium bowl, whisk together the flour, salt, sugar, and baking powder. (If time permits, chill the bowl and flour mixture for 30 minutes before using.) Using the large holes of a grater, grate the frozen lard and butter into the flour mixture. (The frozen fat is easier to incorporate into the dry ingredients and remains cold for a flakier crust.) Using a pastry blender, 2 knives, or your fingertips, work the mixture together until it is crumbly. Add the cheese and mix together. Sprinkle in the ice water, beginning with 4 tablespoons, and mix until the dough holds together when pressed. Shape into 2 disks, wrap in plastic wrap, and chill for 1 hour.

**CHOP THE FROZEN BACON** into bits. (The frozen bacon is easier to chop and doesn't stick together.) In a medium heavy skillet, cook the bacon bits over medium-low heat until they begin to shrink and render some drippings, about 3 minutes. Transfer to a paper towel to drain.

**TO MAKE THE FILLING:** In a large skillet or saucepan, melt the butter over medium-high heat. Add the apples, sugar, cinnamon, and salt. When the apples begin to sizzle, reduce the heat to low, cover, and simmer for 8 minutes. Uncover, increase the heat to medium-high, and cook until the mixture thickens, 5 to 10 minutes. Transfer the filling to a large bowl. Add lemon juice to taste.

**PREHEAT** the oven to 400°F. Line a baking sheet with parchment paper for easy handling, if desired.

**TO ASSEMBLE:** Cut each chilled disk of dough into 4 wedges. Let the wedges warm slightly for easier handling. Shape each into a circle, for a total of 8. To form the bottom crusts, on a lightly floured surface, roll 4 of the wedges into 6-inch circles. To form the top crusts, roll the remaining 4 wedges into slightly larger circles.

**SPRINKLE EACH CIRCLE** with 1 tablespoon bacon bits. Using your fingers, lightly press the bits into the dough. Then lightly roll with a rolling pin.

**TURN THE BOTTOM CRUSTS OVER,** bacon-side down. Spoon $1/2$ cup of the filling onto each bottom crust, leaving a 1-inch border. Brush the edges with water. Cover with 1 of the 4 top crusts, bacon-side up, crimping the edges to seal. Using a sharp paring knife, cut a $1 1/2$-inch long V-shaped vent in the top and peel back. Distribute the remaining bacon bits around the edges of the pies and press into the dough. Trim any rough edges.

**TRANSFER THE PIES** to the baking sheet. Reduce the heat to 350°F and bake until the crusts are golden, about 30 minutes. Transfer to a wire rack and cool until the crusts are just warm to the touch. Serve warm or at room temperature.

**SOURCES**

## Where to Get Top-Quality Bacon

**HIGH-QUALITY,** great-tasting American bacon is out there. The difficulty is finding a selection at your local supermarket or butcher shop. Many small producers either do not have the ability to mass market or choose not to. Some have Web sites, others have mail-order catalogs, and many simply sell to their local markets. It takes a bit of scouting to find the silk purse. This section will help you.

One of the best sources currently on the scene is a mail-order and online enterprise called The Grateful Palate in southern California. The owner, Dan Philips, has an obsession for bacon. Besides more than two dozen artisan-style bacons available by the pound and slab, he features a Bacon-of-the-Month Club.

**THE GRATEFUL PALATE,** Oxnard, CA, (888) 472-5283; www.gratefulpalate.com. Whether you order from the catalog or online, you can access the Grateful Palate's full range of artisan-style bacons. Both are particularly helpful with descriptive tasting notes, prices, and often a photograph so you can make comparisons.

## Here is a list of other bacon sources to help you begin your quest for the best.

**APPLEGATE FARMS,** Branchburg, NJ, (800) 587-5858; www.applegatefarms.com. Their Sunday Bacon, smoked for 12 hours over hardwoods, contains no nitrates. It comes from humanely raised hogs that receive no antibiotics or synthetic growth hormones. (They also carry turkey bacon.) A handy zip code locator lists stores in your area that carry their products.

**GATTON FARMS,** Father's Country Hams, Bremen, KY, (270) 525-3554; www.fatherscountryhams.com. The online store offers bacon and other pork products, plus recipes and an interesting history of the family business. The dry-cured bacon has a remarkably intense flavor and is excellent by itself or in recipes.

**NODINE'S SMOKEHOUSE,** Torrington, CT, (800) 222-2059; www.nodinesmokehouse.com. The online store offers a variety of bacons in half-slabs and slices, including apple-, juniper-, and double-smoked, 10-clove-garlic, and nitrate-free bacons.

**NUESKE'S HILLCREST FARM,** Wittenberg, WI, (800) 392-2266; fax (800) 962-2266; www.nueske.com. This is one of my favorite smoked bacons. It's lean, meaty, and delicious. For more than 60 years, Nueske's Hillcrest Farm has been producing flavorful bacon, cured with brown sugar and honey and smoked over sweet applewood embers. You can order by fax, phone, or online. Nueske's bacon also is available in many supermarkets and butcher shops.

**OSCAR'S BACON,** Warrensburg, NY, (800) 627-3431; www.oscarssmokedmeats.com. Oscar's bacon is cured with salt and honey. No chemicals are used. The online store offers smoked slab, chunk, and sliced Canadian bacon, English, Cajun-style, Texas hot, and an Irish-style bacon cured with Irish whiskey.

**WILLIAM'S BRITISH STYLE MEATS,** Lumberton, NC, (888) 531-3663; www.britishbacon.com. This site offers British-style bacon, boiling bacon, and gammon using the "Wiltshire Cure" method practiced in England for about 200 years. You'll also find an interesting narrative on the history of curing English bacon. Sales are by catalog only.

## Other Sources

**NATIONAL PORK PRODUCERS COUNCIL,** www.porkboard.org, maintains an informative Web site devoted to pork lovers, pork producers, and anyone interested in learning more about pigs and pork. It features recipes, nutritional information, research results, a cooking club, and educational resources. Using their links and a little searching, you can find out how to cure your own bacon.

**RAW PASTEURIZED SHELL EGGS:** Davidson's Pasteurized Shell Eggs, Laconia, NH, www.davidsonseggs.com, undergo the same heating process as milk does to destroy harmful bacteria. To check on the supermarket availability of Davidson's eggs in your area, go to the Web site or call (800) 410-7619. Currently, direct orders are not available.

# INDEX

**131**

# TABLE OF EQUIVALENTS

THE EXACT EQUIVALENTS IN THE FOLLOWING TABLES
HAVE BEEN ROUNDED FOR CONVENIENCE.

## Liquid/Dry Measures

| U.S | METRIC |
|---|---|
| $\frac{1}{4}$ teaspoon | 1.25 milliliters |
| $\frac{1}{2}$ teaspoon | 2.5 milliliters |
| 1 teaspoon | 5 milliliters |
| 1 tablespoon (3 teaspoons) | 15 milliliters |
| 1 fluid ounce (2 tablespoons) | 30 milliliters |
| $\frac{1}{4}$ cup | 60 milliliters |
| $\frac{1}{3}$ cup | 80 milliliters |
| $\frac{1}{2}$ cup | 120 milliliters |
| 1 cup | 240 milliliters |
| 1 pint (2 cups) | 480 milliliters |
| 1 quart (4 cups, 32 ounces) | 960 milliliters |
| 1 gallon (4 quarts) | 3.84 liters |
| | |
| 1 ounce (by weight) | 28 grams |
| 1 pound | 454 grams |
| 2.2 pounds | 1 kilogram |

## Length

| U.S. | METRIC |
|---|---|
| $\frac{1}{8}$ inch | 3 millimeters |
| $\frac{1}{4}$ inch | 6 millimeters |
| $\frac{1}{2}$ inch | 12 millimeters |
| 1 inch | 2.5 centimeters |

## Oven Temperature

| FAHRENHEIT | CELSIUS | GAS |
|---|---|---|
| 250 | 120 | $\frac{1}{2}$ |
| 275 | 140 | 1 |
| 300 | 150 | 2 |
| 325 | 160 | 3 |
| 350 | 180 | 4 |
| 375 | 190 | 5 |
| 400 | 200 | 6 |
| 425 | 220 | 7 |
| 450 | 230 | 8 |
| 475 | 240 | 9 |
| 500 | 260 | 10 |